RECOVERING OUR NERVE

A Primer for Evangelism in Everyday Life

DAVID L. SEBASTIAN

Warner Press

Anderson, Indiana

Coordinator of Publishing & Creative Services
Church of God Ministries, Inc.
PO Box 2420
Anderson, IN 46018-2420
800-848-2464 · www.chog.org

To purchase additional copies of this book, to inquire about distribution, and for all other sales-related matters, please contact:

Warner Press, Inc.
PO Box 2499
Anderson, IN 46018-2499
800-741-7721 · www.warnerpress.org

ISBN: 978-1-59317-655-6

Printed in the United States of America.

13 14 15 16 17 18 / CH / 10 9 8 7 6 5 4 3 2 1

Dedication

To my wife Debbie, and daughters Julie and Amy, you have taught me about the love, justice, and mercy of God.

Contents

Acknowledgments

First of all, as a disciple of Christ, I want to acknowledge Jesus as the way, the truth, and the life.

Over the years, I have been blessed with spiritual giants and exemplary Christian servants along my path. A special thanks to Joseph Allison, who encouraged me to write this book, and to my assistant, Kristen Caylor, and my wife, Debbie Sebastian, for their helpful work on the manuscript.

I am indebted to the following professors and academic institutions for preparing me to embrace the evangelistic mandate: Harold Boyer and Irene Smith Caldwell, of Warner University; Jerry Grubbs, of Anderson University School of Theology; and Eddie Gibbs, William E. Pannell and C. Peter Wagner, of Fuller Theological Seminary. I am grateful for the partnership in the gospel with the ministers in daily life at Church at the Crossing (Glendale), Indianapolis, Indiana; North Hills Church of God, Phoenix, Arizona; and Salem Church of God, Clayton, Ohio. A special appreciation is extended to President James Edwards for his empowering leadership and his call to me to serve as dean and to Anderson University School of Theology colleagues and students for their commitment to the ministry of biblical reconciliation.

Last, but not least, I am deeply grateful for the invitation from David Grubbs to attend a lay-witness training event in Dayton, Ohio, in 1971. Little did I know that invitation would change the direction of my life.

Falling in Love
with the Story

I will never forget the evening my friend stopped by my place of business. We were in our early twenties, and both of us had returned home from our time in military service. Our friendship had started in the sixth grade. He attended church with me on several occasions because I had invited him to play on the church basketball and softball teams. One requirement of participation was to attend church services during the season, at the least, so my friend attended sporadically. His family had never attended church.

I am not sure how our conversation turned to spiritual matters, but at one point my friend asked, "How do you become a Christian?"

I do not remember exactly what I said, but I was not ready to give a reason for the hope I had within (1 Pet 3:15). Some might console me by saying, "What was important was the conversation, not whether you answered his question." I disagree. I do believe that people are drawn to Christ by the Holy Spirit, not as a result of our effective arguments; however, when given the opportunity, I was ill-equipped to help a friend take a first step with Christ.

Soon after that uncomfortable evening, a pastor from a neighboring community spoke to the men's group at my home church. He invited us to attend a lay-witness training event where people would learn how to share their faith. The law of educational readiness was at work, so I signed up immediately. I took further evangelism training with Campus Crusade for Christ (CRU). The evangelism training I received, with all of its strengths and weaknesses, changed the direction of my life.

As a result of that training, I began actively witnessing to family, friends, and strangers. I eventually sold my business and enrolled in college, then seminary. While in seminary, I served a congregation as the minister of evangelism and Christian education; after seminary, I became a senior pastor for eighteen years and was involved in planting four new churches. I also served my state organization by being a member of a church-planting task force. Over the years, I have been equipped to communicate the gospel through the ministries of Campus Crusade, Evangelism Explosion, Willow Creek Association, the American Institute for Church Growth, Natural Church Development, and the Alpha Course. I also chose to pursue my doctor of ministry in theology degree with a concentration in evangelism.

I share this background, not to tout my credentials, but to recount how my interest in evangelism has grown across the years. I have fallen in love with the gospel of the kingdom of God and have given forty years of my life to disciple-making.

For the past fifteen years, as dean of Anderson University School of Theology, I have taught a course titled "Evangelism in the Local Church." This course began as an elective in the curriculum but has now become a required course, due to our ongoing program assessment in which our seminary graduates indicated the need for a required course in evangelism.[1] My prayer is that all of our graduates will become "fishers of women and men" and establish ministries of multiplication.

Of course, the way we do evangelism will change from time to time. Some methods of evangelism are only effective for a season, and some approaches to evangelism are effective only in particular

---

1. John Aukerman, director of outcomes assessment and distance education, Report to the Faculty Regarding the Master of Divinity Degree, 2007.

cultural contexts. Methods change but the message remains. The Great Commission to "go and make disciples" never allows us to sit and make excuses," even when our story has been hijacked by "conservative reductionism or liberal embarrassment."[2] I trust each generation will be motivated to take seriously the call to make disciples. Those who embrace this calling have the promise that Christ will minister with them, "even to the end of the age" (Matt 28:20 NKJV).

In one way, the following pages are a reflective practicum on evangelism that began with the question of my friend: "How do I become a Christian?" That question is simple yet profound. It was asked on the day of Pentecost: "When the people heard this, they were cut to the heart and said to Peter and the other apostles, 'Brothers, what shall we do?'" (Acts 2:37). I trust this book will equip you to answer that question, and to explore what it means to communicate the gospel of the kingdom of God in an emerging culture. Yes, our strategies will look different from the first century or even the twentieth century but the gospel story must be told. One poet expressed it this way:

I love to tell the story of unseen things above,
Of Jesus and His glory, of Jesus and His love;
I love to tell the story because I know 'tis true,
It satisfies my longing as nothing else can do.
I love to tell the story! 'Twill be my theme in glory
To tell the old, old story of Jesus and his love.[3]

2. Brueggemann, *Biblical Perspectives on Evangelism*, 14.

3. Katherine Hankey and William G. Fischer, "I Love to Tell the Story," in *Worship the Lord: Hymnal of the Church of God* (Anderson, IN: Warner Press, 1989), 361.

Chapter One

Centering Salvation in the Cosmic Story

Every great story has a plot. A *plot* is the central idea of a narrative that unfolds over a period of time. A captivating story also has a *context*, the setting in which key characters are introduced and developed. Characters in a story generally encounter a problem that needs to be resolved. A resolved story offers a degree of satisfaction where all wrongs are made right and "all live happily ever after."

The story about Jesus Christ as God's Son and our Savior only makes sense if understood in relation to the bigger story that unfolds in the Scripture. Frank Viola, in an interview about his book *From Eternity to Here,* notes that before the fall and even before creation, "God's relentless, eternal, and ultimate desire"[1] was made known. The apostle Paul writes concerning this, "Praise be to the God and Father of our Lord Jesus Christ, who has blessed us in the heavenly realms with every spiritual blessing in Christ. For he chose us in him before the creation of the world, to be holy and blameless" (Eph 1:3–4). "The Son is the image of the invisible God, the firstborn over all creation. For in him all things were created: things in heaven and on earth, visible and invisible, whether thrones or powers or rulers or authorities; all things have

1. Viola, Frank. "'Christianity Today' Interview: God's Grand Mission," *Beyond Evangelical* (blog), June 11, 2009, http://frankviola.org/2009/06/11/christianity -today-interview/.

been created through him and for him. He is before all things, and in him all things hold together" (Col 1:15–17).

This cosmic story of God's eternal desire to be in relationship with all creatures and creation provides the context for the Jesus story. Indeed, the Jesus story brings resolution to God's desire and dilemma of the need for reconciliation with all of estranged creation. The cosmic story of salvation past, present, and future unfolds in four acts.

Act One: Creation

The story begins with God, who existed eternally before creation. Every created thing emanated from the Godhead and was good (Gen 1:31). On the sixth day of creation, human beings were made. Human beings were in many ways similar to other sixth-day "soulish" creatures but with a marked difference: Humans were created in the image of God (Gen 1:27) and were set apart for a divine purpose. Woman and man were progenitors of the human race and God's partners in overseeing all of creation (Gen 1:28). They were placed in Paradise, and in Paradise all lived in peace. Creatures large and small lived as created beings in the garden of God. At first, everything God created was good and all lived in harmony.

Act Two: Crisis

However, one day the "tempter speaking through the voice of a serpent"[2] came to the woman and said, "Did God really say, 'You must not eat from any tree in the garden'?" (Gen 3:1). The woman said, "No, we have the freedom to eat from any tree except the one tree in the middle of the garden." That tree, according to

---

2. Bonhoeffer, *Creation and Fall*, 66–67.

God's command, was off-limits. It could have been a lake, path, or mountain, but in the Genesis hymn of creation, one tree was off-limits. Everything in Paradise was accessible to humankind but this one thing. Human disobedience, not the devil, caused the cosmic disruption.

The serpent tempted the woman to subtly doubt the word of God. "You will not certainly die, the serpent said to the woman" (Gen 3:4). She took and ate the fruit, and then gave some to her husband. They looked at each other and realized, "We are still alive. The serpent was right. We did not die." The man and woman had to choose between two accounts of reality, and they chose to believe the lie of the serpent rather than to trust and obey the Word of God.

This deliberate act of disobedience caused a cataclysmic rupture in creation. When they succumbed to the temptation to experience life on their own terms, something happened beyond human comprehension, but something nonetheless real. As a result, the man (Adam) and the woman (Eve) were exiled from Paradise (Gen 3:24). Their relationship with God was broken. Their egalitarian partnership was compromised. Their ability to oversee creation was diminished. Paradise was lost.

Act Three: Covenant

Although Paradise was lost, God was not finished. The tempter had won the battle but not the war. God intended to reconcile all things to himself. God would accomplish this reconciliation through a covenant people who would live in harmony with the Creator, cosmos, and creation.

Abram (Abraham) would become the father of a people who, through faith and faithfulness, would be a light unto all the nations (Gen 12:2–3). In the course of time, the people of God became enslaved. God raised up a servant named Moses, who would liberate Israel and give them the Law as a guide for the holy life

God intended. The Law exposed their sin but could not excise sin. Innocent animals were sacrificed almost daily to atone for Israel's sin (Lev 16). These repeated sacrifices reminded the Israelites of the seriousness of their transgression, but could not release them from its power over their lives. Therefore God, in the fullness time (Gal 4:4), entered into the world by taking on human flesh. Jesus the Christ shared in our humanity (Heb 2:14–16) and made a final atonement for our sin by freely giving himself as a ransom to all who would believe in him (Heb 9:15). The death and resurrection of Jesus broke the power of cancelled sin.

Act Four: Consummation

Jesus began the reign of God on earth. His advent ushered in what have been called the "last days" of this world as we know it (Heb 1:1–2). Through his birth, life, and ministry he began to establish the kind of existence on earth that God had in mind from the beginning. Jesus called women and men to serve, teach, and fellowship in his name. He died on the cross as a sacrifice for sin, as a release from bondage to the evil one and as an example of a loving life lived for God and others. The resurrection of Jesus confirmed to his followers that he has overcome death and now sits at the right hand of God (his accession).

The cosmic story reminds us that one day Jesus will return (Acts 1:11). When Jesus returns, he will come to judge the living and the dead in order to establish a new heaven and earth. The righteous will be with Jesus and the unrighteous will be separated from him forever (Matt 25:34, 41, 46). Until his second coming, he has commissioned his followers to "go and make disciples of all nations, baptizing them in the name of the Father and of the Son and of the Holy Spirit, and teaching them to obey everything I have commanded you" (Matt 18:19–21). And Jesus has promised, "Surely I am with you always, to the very end of the age" (v 21).

The cosmic story of salvation—understood as creation, crisis, covenant, and consummation—can be the defining narrative around which we order our lives. In all its ancientness, the old story has the power to transform life. All people live by some story, whether or not they know it. Some live by this story:

Row, row, row your boat
gently down the stream...
Merrily, merrily, merrily, merrily,
life is but a dream.

Others live by the narrative, "Eat, drink, and be merry, for tomorrow you die." Still others embrace the saga:

Que sera, sera,
Whatever will be, will be.[3]

Walter Brueggemann, a noted biblical scholar, reminds us that "evangelism is inviting people into these stories (biblical narratives) as the definitional story of our life, and thereby authorizing people to give up, abandon, and renounce other stories that have shaped their lives in false or distorting ways."[4] Evangelism is about inviting people to take a first step into the gospel story. All human stories have truth claims, and disciples of Jesus lovingly and respectfully share the truth claim of Jesus as the way, the truth, and the life. Some people will embrace that story and others will reject it. Our task is not to coerce people into accepting the truth claims of Jesus' story. Our task as evangelists is to recover our nerve and tell that story authentically through our words and deeds.

---

3. "Que Sera, Sera (Whatever Will Be, Will Be)," lyrics and music by Jay Livingston and Ray Evans. © 1956.

4. Brueggemann, *Biblical Perspectives on Evangelism*, 10.

Chapter Two
Telling the Gospel Story Accurately

Ron Sider poses an important question about the gospel: "Is it more biblical to summarize the Good News as the Good News of forgiveness or as the Good News of the Kingdom of God?"[1] Sider reminds us that "the vast majority of New Testament scholars today, whether evangelical or liberal, agree that the central aspect of Jesus' teachings was the gospel of the Kingdom of God. The words 'kingdom of God' or Matthew's equivalent, 'kingdom of heaven' appear 122 times in Matthew, Mark and Luke, and 92 times they are on the lips of Jesus himself."[2] Several interpreters of the gospel story oversimplify the good news of the kingdom of God to the point that they offer us something that resembles the gospel of the kingdom but not the good news itself. The gospel of the kingdom is simple but not simplistic.

Exposing a Reductionist Gospel

One such view understands the gospel to be exclusively the forgiveness of sins. In this view, the mission of the church is to help people acknowledge that they are sinners in need of the saving grace of God. The goal of evangelism is to help people understand that they are dead in their trespasses and sins, to help them pray the sinner's prayer in order to receive the gift of eternal life, and to assure people of heaven when they die. Getting people ready

---

1. Sider, Good News and Good Works, 30.
2. Sider, Scandal of the Evangelical Conscience, 60–61.

for heaven is gospel work, and certainly we all need to be saved from the penalty of our sins, but this is not the whole truth of the gospel.

Another oversimplified view of the gospel contends that it's all about working for the righteousness of God in the here and now. The good news is not so much about getting people into heaven as it is about getting heaven into people. People who hold this view feel that the gospel is about working for the peaceful reign (*shalom*) of God by giving drink to the thirsty, feeding the hungry, clothing the naked, and providing care for widows and orphans. They contend that the gospel of the kingdom is also about exposing unjust social and political structures in order to create a culture of fairness and righteousness for all, especially the poor and marginalized. Certainly, this view contains an important truth because "faith without works is dead" (James 2:17), but it falls far short of encompassing the whole of God's good news.

A third view of the gospel might be called the members-only version, because it understands that church growth is the essence of kingdom work. According to this view, the Christian mission is to invite new people to join the church and become responsible members of it—paying tithes, attending services, and supporting the pastoral staff in doing the work of the kingdom. Occasionally, laypersons are encouraged to be involved in new-member campaigns, in which they invite their friends, families, and business associates to attend public worship services. If visitors are not members of any church (or if they are lapsed members), then they are invited to a membership class where they are given opportunity to be incorporated into the congregation as full members. Certainly, Christians are not to be isolated believers. Scripture encourages us to "spur one another on toward love and good deeds, not giving up meeting together, as some are in the habit of doing" (Heb 10:25), but evangelism is not merely a church-member transfer system.

Each of these reductionist models of the gospel has an element of truth. The gospel is about sinners' being saved by grace through faith. The gospel is about redeemed people working for righteousness and justice on earth as it is in heaven. A gospel community is one in which reconciled people gather regularly in large and small groups for instruction, fellowship, and service. The gospel of the kingdom includes all three components.

Notice that our understanding of the good news will determine what we think evangelism means. Walter Brueggemann writes, "The noun *gospel*, which means message, is linked in the Bible to the verb *tell-the-news* (one word *bissar*, in Hebrew)."[3] Therefore, evangelism is telling the good news about Jesus and joining his community in making this world a better place while preparing for the world to come.

Today, most assuredly, the theological term *evangelism* has its own cultural baggage. It evokes images that may hold people back from communicating the gospel with others. However, again in the words of Bruegemann, we need to "recover nerve about our modes of speech in church traditions that have debased our speech, either by conservative reductionism or by liberal embarrassment."[4] We also need to avoid the false dichotomy of evangelism versus social action.[5] Reclaiming evangelism for our time requires us to embrace a holistic understanding of the call to make disciples. The following is a working definition of evangelism that attempts to express such an understanding:

Evangelism is communicating in word and deed the liberating power of the gospel and, through the guidance of the Holy Spirit, inviting people to repent of sin, to be baptized in the

---

3. Brueggemann, *Biblical Perspectives on Evangelism*, 14.
4. Ibid.
5. Ibid., 43.

name of the triune God, confessing Jesus as Savior and Lord, and to be incorporated into the church as the visible expression of the kingdom of God in this age and the age to come.

This definition could be expressed as I^3 Evangelism. I^3 Evangelism has three components:

1. Incarnational Evangelism
2. Invitational Evangelism
3. Incorporational Evangelism

Chapter Three

The Incarnational Gospel

Saint Francis of Assisi is reported to have said to his fellow monks, "Preach the gospel at all times, and if necessary use words." Saint Francis emphasized an important component of the gospel of the kingdom: our being the presence of Christ in our world.

Incarnational Evangelism is about the whole of the disciple's life communicating the whole life of Jesus. Sometimes the gospel is thought to be encapsulated in Passion Week, when Jesus suffered, died, and rose again. However, the good news began before the foundation of the world and continued with his birth and earthly ministry. Luke records that "God anointed Jesus of Nazareth with the Holy Spirit and power...and he went around doing good and healing all who were under the power of the devil, because God was with him" (Acts 10:38).

The theological term *incarnational evangelism* denotes this idea that evangelism is our being the presence of Christ in the world. While the word *incarnation* is not in the Bible, it communicates the biblical teaching that God took on human form and, in the words of John, "made his dwelling among us" (John 1:14). Incarnational evangelism underscores the fact that Jesus' disciples continue to do his work by being his eyes, hands, and feet in the present world. The incarnational component of the gospel is expressed in the prophetic words of Jesus:

> "Not everyone who says to me, 'Lord, Lord,' will enter into the kingdom of heaven, but only those who do the will of my Father who is in heaven." (Matt 7:21)

"Come, you who are blessed by my Father; take your inheritance, the kingdom prepared for you since the creation of the world. For I was hungry and you gave me something to eat, I was thirsty and you gave me something to drink, I was a stranger and you invited me in, I needed clothes and you clothed me, I was sick and you looked after me, I was in prison and you came to visit me." (Matt 25:34–36)

Incarnational evangelism often takes the form of what John Perkins describes as relief, development and structural change.[1] *Relief* is coming to the aid of people in times of social disaster by providing food, housing, and other essentials to help them survive. *Development* is helping people access resources, education, and expertise so they can help themselves and others. *Structural change* is working for permanent social transformation through legislation, political process, and economic justice so that all people can have the freedom of opportunity. In many ways, incarnational evangelism is a reaction against a style of evangelism that only seeks to proclaim the words of Jesus; it insists that the deeds of Jesus must also be evident in evangelism.

Pastor Frank Ward is an urban minister in the city of Chicago, Illinois. He founded Matthew 25:40, a ministry with senior adults in uptown Chicago. The congregation that Pastor Ward serves consists of poor senior citizens who find it almost impossible to get out of their apartments for food, medicine, and other basic human needs. Pastor Ward advocates basic human rights for what the Bible calls "the least of these" (Matt 25:40). If the ministry of Pastor Ward would cease, there would be an immediate outcry from the community, because he represents the eyes, hands, and feet of God. "How beautiful on the mountains are the feet of those who bring good news" (Isa 52:7).

---

1. Sider, *Good News and Good Works*, 138.

In Washington, DC, Pastor Cheryl Sanders is a scholar and pastor who serves as the lead minister of the Third Street Church of God. In addition to her long tenure at Third Street, Dr. Sanders serves as professor of Christian ethics at Howard Divinity School. Over the years, the church has hosted an urban prayer breakfast that provides worship and a meal for people on the streets and those staying in local shelters. The meal is not served in a soup kitchen but a place where folks can come and sit together and study the Bible. In addition, the church operates a clothing distribution program and a tutoring and counseling service. The church is a voice of reconciliation for those living in the District of Columbia. Dr. Sanders is invited to speak in the halls of power in the nation's capital because, as a pastor and professor, she advocates for justice and speaks a prophetic word to our elected officials.

These are just two examples of incarnational evangelism, and our world is full of them. Dennis F. Kinlaw boldly declares it in the title of his book *We Live as Christ.* He writes:

This is what Paul meant when he said, "For me, to live is Christ" (Phil. 1:21). I've always been impressed by that verse and wanted to use it as my life verse, but I was afraid it might seem a bit arrogant. For me to live, that is Christ? Sure, Christ is life for me. But this also means that I am to be Christ to other people...Paul says this without a blink.[2]

Evangelism means first of all that we become Christ for other people. We touch them in comfort, correction, and guidance. When we see someone in need, we do not simply ask, "What would Jesus do?" We are Christ in the midst of their situation.

---

2. Kinlaw, *We Live as Christ,* 24.

Chapter Four

The Invitational Gospel

Invitational Evangelism also involves proclaiming the words of the gospel. Walter Brueggemann reminds us that "at the center of the act of evangelism is the message announced, a verbal, out-loud assertion of something decisive not known until this moment of utterance."[1] In order for evangelism to be holistic, it must not only do but also proclaim (speak) the words of the gospel.

The Greek word *kerygma* literally means "to proclaim." While *kerygma* is not the only word in the New Testament associated with the task of sharing the good news, it is the word most often utilized. Over time, the word *kerygma* has also come to mean the message that was preached by the earliest evangelists. *Kerygma* in this sense has to do with the content of the good news that is to be communicated far and wide. It was not enough for the apostles simply to do the loving deeds that Jesus modeled for his followers. People of the good news were to testify to the meaning of Christ's life, death, and resurrection. A holistic communication of the atoning work of Christ on the cross[2], including his bodily resurrection from the grave, maintains guard against a reductionist interpretation of the gospel, for "all reductions of the Gospel are wrong."[3]

In 1 Corinthians 15, we have the oldest and most detailed account of the resurrection found in Scripture. Before the apostle Paul writes about the future resurrection of the Christian believer,

---

1. Brueggemann, *Biblical Perspectives on Evangelism*, 14.
2. A holistic interpretation of the atonement embraces all New Testament metaphors. See Baker and Green, *Recovering the Scandal of the Cross*, for a study of New Testament metaphors of the atonement.
3. Belcher, *Deep Church*, 112.

he establishes in 1 Corinthians 15:1–8 the historical content of the gospel. The apostle reminds the Corinthians of several essentials: **First, the gospel is to be passed on.** Paul does not see himself as the author of the gospel, but a faithful steward of the message he received. Therefore, he exhorts the followers of Jesus to get the story straight and then faithfully pass it on. "Now brothers and sisters, I want to remind you of the gospel I preached to you, which you received and on which you have taken your stand. By this gospel you are saved, if you hold firmly to the word I preached to you. Otherwise you have believed in vain" (1 Cor 15:1–2).

Second, the gospel content is to be preserved. "For what I received I passed on to you as of first importance: that Christ died for our sins according to the Scriptures, that he was buried, that he was raised on the third day according to the Scriptures, and that he appeared to Cephas and then to the Twelve" (1 Cor 15:3–7). Gordon Fee notes that the content of the gospel can be summed up in four short clauses[4]:

Christ died to take away our sins. This language is reflective of the atoning sacrifice described in Leviticus 16. Isaiah 53 describes the one who, as a lamb led to slaughter, took away the sins of the people (Isa 53:7). Judaism did not necessarily interpret Isaiah 53 as a prophesy regarding the Messiah but understood these words to describe the Persian King Cyrus as God's anointed one to bring about the restoration of Israel.[5] Gordon Fee suggests the person who did link Jesus with Isaiah 53 must be considered the founder of Christianity. Fee contends that Jesus, in the upper room prior to his death and resurrection, points to himself as this reality in the institution of the last supper (1 Cor 11:23–25). Since we are separated from God because of our sin(s), the death of Christ on the cross is essential for our salvation.

---

4. Fee, *First Epistle to the Corinthians*, 717.
5. *Interpreter's Dictionary of The Bible*, 1:755.

Christ died for our sins according to the Scriptures. The phrase "according to the Scriptures" does not refer to a single verse or a set of passages but to the Hebrew Scriptures as a whole. The Scriptures remind us that when Adam and Eve sinned, God provided a covering for their shame with animal skin (Gen 3:21). Abraham was instructed to sacrifice his only son Isaac, but instead God provided a substitute ram for the sacrifice (Gen 22). In the Exodus, the blood of a spotless lamb was smeared on the door frames of Israelite homes so the Lord would pass over them and spare the firstborn of the Jews (Ex 12). This shedding of blood, in turn, became part of the sacrificial system in which animals bore the sins of the people on the Day of Atonement. On the cross Jesus would become the perfect and final sacrifice.

That he was buried. The gospel reminds us that a dead corpse was laid in the grave so that the resurrection that followed would be recognized as an objective reality, not merely a spiritual phenomenon. Some who denied the bodily resurrection contended that Jesus did not actually die but rather fainted. Others contended that Jesus, left for dead, resuscitated and reappeared. But the gospel record affirms that Jesus actually died and was buried.

Christ was raised on the third day. The phrase that "he was raised" (perfect passive) reminds the reader that Jesus was raised (a past historical event) and still lives (a present reality). According to the Scriptures, "He appeared to Cephas, and then to the Twelve. After that, he appeared to more than five hundred of the brothers and sisters at the same time, most of whom are still living, though some have fallen asleep" (1 Cor 15:5–6). By describing the resurrection of Jesus as "the first fruit" (1 Cor 15:23), Scripture assures believers of a resurrected body in the life to come as well as resurrection power for living today.

Third, personal experience is part of the good news. Christ was experienced by those who chose to believe. Saul of Tarsus opposed the way of Jesus, but one day the light of the gospel broke into his life (Acts 9:1–19; 22:3–16; 26:9–18). As he described it, "And last of all he appeared to me also, as to one abnormally born" (1 Cor 15:8). Gordon Fee reminds us that the Greek term *ektroma,* translated "abnormally born," traditionally has been understood to mean that Paul recognized his own experience to be outside the normal process. In other words, he did not come to know Christ as the other apostles did. However, this is not the only way to translate *ektroma. "Ektroma* is a Greek word that also can be translated as 'miscarriage' or 'abortion' and possibly refers to his 'lowly' status as 'least' among the apostles, which was perhaps hurled at him as an epithet by some of the Corinthians."[6]

Paul undoubtedly had to deal with his vain regrets of the past and his fear for the future. However, a transformed Paul would go on to write, "I am not ashamed of the gospel, because it is the power of God that brings salvation to everyone who believes: first to the Jew, then to the Gentile" (Rom 1:16). The call to experience the gospel is a vital component of invitational evangelism.

The Rock Church in San Diego, California, is committed to the proclamation of the gospel. Pastor Miles McPherson, a former professional football player, began evangelistic Bible studies on the campus of San Diego State University, a ministry that eventually birthed The Rock Church. Pastor McPherson's sermons end with an invitation for people who do not know Jesus to come forward and make a public profession of faith. Each person who comes forward is assigned a prayer partner who counsels them in regard to next steps in Christian discipleship. Every message, regardless of the subject matter, ends with an invitation to nonbelievers to take the first step in embracing the gospel.

Another proclamation model of evangelism is the Alpha Course. The Alpha Course invites people to come and explore what the Christian faith is all about and have fun at the same time.

---

6. Fee, *First Epistle to the Corinthians,* 719.

There is a common meal, a time of instruction, and then questions are shared in small groups. No question is off-limits. God is using this ministry to help people discover what it means to be a follower of Christ and give them the opportunity to follow Jesus. The Alpha Course is committed to teaching people about the life changes that occur when people embrace the gospel.

Chapter Five

The Incorporational Gospel

As the early church formally and informally proclaimed the gospel message, they also "persuaded"[1] hearers to repent, be baptized and be incorporated into the company of the committed. The task of the evangelist was not to manipulate people's emotions or pressure them to make a decision, but rather to encourage a positive response to the work of the Holy Spirit. The early evangelists were convinced that the Holy Spirit went before them, preparing the hearts of people to believe the message and be incorporated into the church of Jesus.

Portraits of Incorporation: A Trilogy

The gospel of Matthew reported the teaching of Jesus regarding the new community of the faithful, which he called the *ecclesia* or "church" (Matt 16:18). Matthew 1–12 chronicles the work of Jesus inaugurating the kingdom of God. Growing communities of belongers observed his compassion and were benefactors of his deeds. They heard his teaching regarding a new day in which the will of God would be done on earth as it is in heaven. The crowds were invited to participate in all Jesus had to offer.

Beginning in chapter 13, there is a transition in the way Matthew describes these people. Rather than simply being a crowd that followed Jesus, they started to become the church of Jesus. Chapters 13–28 of Matthew are sometimes referred

---

1. The Greek word *patho* describes the intent to persuade church belongers to become believers, as seen in Acts 13:43; 17:4; 18:4; and 28:23–24.

to as the "church book."[2] The New Testament's teaching on the church reaches a crescendo in Matthew 16:16–18, where Peter confesses, "You are the Messiah, the son of the living God." The response of Christ is, "You are Peter, and on this rock I will build my church, and the gates of Hades will not overcome it."

The pericopes of Matthew 21:28–32; Matthew 21:33–46; and Matthew 22:1–14 present a trilogy of parables portraying that members of the *ecclesia* (church) will consist of both Jew and Gentile. Jesus uses a literary device known as parable. Parables are not just about information but are always about transformation. These three parables challenge belongers to understand what it means to become believers and members of the church. Through these three parables Jesus helps us understand what incorporational evangelism is intended to be.

Portrait: Obedience to the Father

The Parable of the Two Sons (Matt 21:28–32)

"What do you think? There was a man who had two sons. He went to the first and said, 'Son, go and work today in the vineyard.'

"'I will not,' he answered, but later he changed his mind and went.

"Then the father went to the other son and said the same thing. He answered, 'I will, sir,' but he did not go.

"Which of the two did what his father wanted?"

"The first," they answered.

Jesus said to them, "Truly I tell you, the tax collectors and the prostitutes are entering the kingdom of God ahead of you. For John came to you to show you the way of righteousness,

---

2. Brunner, *Matthew, A Commentary*, 771.

Recovering Our Nerve

and you did not believe him, but the tax collectors and the prostitutes did. And even after you saw this, you did not repent and believe him.

The parable of the two sons reminds Jesus' followers it is not enough to simply talk the talk. Membership in the church of Jesus is living in obedience to the word of the Father. And when followers realize they are not living in obedience, they must repent and do the will of the Father. Jesus noted, prostitutes and tax collectors, who were also part of the community following Jesus, were repenting and changing their ways, yet the thoroughly religious, who were also following Jesus, were unwilling to change their ways. Mike Breen, an Anglican clergyman, has said, "Christian discipleship is not complex and easy but simple and hard." Incorporated disciples are those who do the work of the Father.

Portrait: Loyal to the Son

The Parable of the Tenants (Matt 21:33–46)

"Listen to another parable: There was a landowner who planted a vineyard. He put a wall around it, dug a winepress in it and built a watchtower. Then he rented the vineyard to some farmers and moved to another place. When the harvest time approached, he sent his servants to the tenants to collect his fruit.

"The tenants seized his servants; they beat one, killed another, and stoned a third. Then he sent other servants to them, more than the first time, and the tenants treated them the same way. Last of all, he sent his son to them. 'They will respect my son,' he said.

"But when the tenants saw the son, they said to each other, 'This is the heir. Come, let's kill him and take his inheritance.' So they took him and threw him out of the vineyard and killed him.

"Therefore, when the owner of the vineyard comes, what will he do to those tenants?"

"He will bring those wretches to a wretched end," they replied, "And he will rent the vineyard to other tenants, who will give him his share of the crop at harvest time."

Jesus said to them, "Have you never read in the Scriptures:

"'The stone the builders rejected
     has become the cornerstone;
the Lord has done this,
     and it is marvelous in our eyes'?

"Therefore I tell you that the kingdom of God will be taken away from you and given to a people who will produce its fruit. Anyone who falls on this stone will be broken to pieces; anyone on whom it falls will be crushed."

When the chief priests and the Pharisees heard Jesus' parables, they knew he was talking about them. They looked for a way to arrest him, but they were afraid of the crowd because the people held that he was a prophet.

The second parable of the trilogy portrays two kinds of tenants and helps the followers of Jesus understand the fate of those who reject the Son. True disciples are those who welcome the Son to his rightful place in the life of the kingdom. Matthew identifies Jesus as the Son who becomes the chief cornerstone on which everything will rise or fall (Matt 21:33–45). Jesus is the foundation of the church. Therefore the church confesses:

At the beginning of time God created humankind to be partners in mission. However, humankind failed in this partnership.

In the course of time, though, God chose Israel to bless all peoples. But in the fullness of time it was in Jesus Christ that God brought salvation for all people. And until the end of time God has chosen the church to be the body of Christ with the mission of making disciples.[3]

For many years, the Christian church has interpreted the parable of the tenants to mean judgment on Israel who failed to allow Jesus the Messiah to have his rightful place. Therefore, God removed Israel from her place as "a light unto the nations" and set the church in its place. But as the new Israel, consisting of both Jew and Gentile, has the church failed to realize the punch of the parable? John Calvin once asserted, "If God had been compelled to change tenants once, he could if provoked, do it again."[4] In a pluralistic culture that is becoming increasingly committed to pluralism, the particularity of Jesus Christ must not be marginalized. With great humility and reverence, the church confesses Jesus as Lord.

Portrait: Righteous living by the Spirit

The Parable of the Wedding Banquet (Matt 22:1–14)

Jesus spoke to them again in parables, saying: "The kingdom of heaven is like a king who prepared a wedding banquet for his son. He sent his servants to those who had been invited to the banquet to tell them to come, but they refused to come.

"Then he sent some more servants and said, 'Tell those who have been invited that I have prepared my dinner: My oxen

---

3. Anderson University School of Theology Faculty, *We Believe*, 7–8.
4. Brunner, *Matthew, A Commentary*, 77.

and fattened cattle have been butchered, and everything is ready. Come to the wedding banquet.'

"But they paid no attention and went off—one to his field, another to his business. The rest seized his servants, mistreated them and killed them. The king was enraged. He sent his army and destroyed those murderers and burned their city.

"Then he said to his servants, 'The wedding banquet is ready, but those I invited did not deserve to come. So go to the street corners and invite to the banquet anyone you find.' So the servants went out into the streets and gathered all the people they could find, the bad as well as the good, and the wedding hall was filled with guests.

"But when the king came in to see the guests, he noticed a man there who was not wearing wedding clothes. He asked, 'How did you get in here without wedding clothes, friend?' The man was speechless.

"Then the king told the attendants, 'Tie him hand and foot, and throw him outside, into the darkness, where there will be weeping and gnashing of teeth.'

"For many are invited, but few are chosen."

The third parable of the trilogy portrays two kinds of wedding guests and alerts us to the fact that "many are invited, but few are chosen" (v 14). According to this parable, those who have responded to the invitation and willingly wear the wedding garment are incorporated into the festivities. St. Augustine interpreted the required wedding garment as love. Martin Luther regarded the garment as justifying faith. However, Fredrick Brunner reminds us that the wedding garment of Matthew is not to be confused with the love of 1 Corinthians 13 or the justification by faith described in Ephesians 2. Brunner writes, "The wedding garment, in the context of the Gospel of Matthew, is to be understood as righteousness and not a passive, imputed righteousness; but an active, moral life."[5] It is the kind of righteousness Jesus had in mind when he called people to live up to that which they know. "Unless your righteousness surpasses that of the Pharisees and the teachers of the law, you will certainly not enter the kingdom of heaven" (Matt 5:20). It is the kind of righteousness that will stand divine scrutiny, for "on that day many will say, 'Lord, Lord,' but I will say, 'Depart from me; I never knew you'" (Matt 7:21, paraphrase).

Now it is imperative to understand that in the parable of the wedding garment, righteousness was not necessary to be invited to the banquet. Jesus did not require the crowds that followed him to do anything but observe his deeds and hear his parables. However, for those he called to enter the church, he raised the bar. The parable taught all are invited, but the garment (of righteousness) was necessary to stay at the banquet. Jesus called belongers to become believers. Jack Stackhouse, a theology professor at Regent College, laments that "some believers are a bit like the perpetual adolescent Christian. Perpetual adolescent Christians are those who lie, cheat and otherwise sin against others with an attitude of 'I'm-cool-cause-Jesus-loves-me-and-so-I-don't-owe-you-a-thing.'"[6]

Followers are incorporated into the life of the church by being obedient to the word of the Father, loyal to the one and only Son, and empowered by the Spirit to live holy and righteous lives. Pastor Dietrich Bonhoeffer (1906–45), in his classic book *The Cost of Discipleship,* called the church of his day to renounce cheap grace and be incorporated into a community of discipleship in contrast to a nominal church membership.

A good example of this incorporational model, in which the church calls belongers to become believers, is found at The Church at Brook Hills, in Birmingham, Alabama. Pastor David Platt is unleashing his people to become a radical community of

---

5. Ibid.
6. Sider, *Scandal of the Evangelical Conscience,* 57.

disciple makers. He believes that many Christians have become accustomed to a tame Americanized Christianity that has nothing in common with authentic discipleship as seen in the New Testament. "I believe that God has uniquely created every one of his people to impact the world," he says. "Some may count it as idealistic, but I believe it is thoroughly biblical, rooted in Psalm 67:1–2, yet covering Scripture from beginning to end. God is in the business of blessing his people so that his ways and his salvation might be made known among all people."[7]

To learn more about incorporational evangelism, i.e., evangelism through the local church, visit www.radical.net. The purpose of Radical.net is to awaken a passion for the glory of God in all nations by encouraging and equipping Christians and churches to accomplish the Great Commission.

---

7. "Meet Our Pastor, accessed July 15, 2013, http://www.brookhills.org/new/pastor.html.

Recovering Our Nerve

Chapter Six

Discerning the Emerging Culture

Many have written prophetically concerning a major cultural shift of our time and the way this shift is changing the way we do evangelism. Certainly the church is not immune to these cultural shifts. One writer has observed,

> from time to time the only way to understand what is currently happening to us as twenty-first-century Christians in North America is first to understand about every five hundred years the church feels compelled to hold a gigantic rummage sale... we are now living in and through one of those five-hundred-year sales.[1]

Phyllis Tickle reminds us that any ministry ideas, programs, and preferences that are no longer effective must periodically be moved to the curb and new approaches to ministry and mission must be embraced. This change is not something to be feared. In fact, it appears that God may use these seismic shifts as opportunities to communicate divine intent.

The change currently taking place in the Western world is commonly described as a move from the modern world to the postmodern world. Therefore, the task of a Christian evangelist is not only to build bridges from the ancient world to the modern world but to build bridges across the pre-modern, modern, and postmodern divides. It is important to remember that while

---

1. Tickle, *Great Emergence*, 16.

the postmodern world is emerging, the modern world has not passed away, nor will it meet its demise in the current generation. Christians who are committed to the ministry of multiplying disciples through the church must become knowledgeable, if not comfortable, in all three worlds and whatever world we might see just beyond the horizon.

The Pre-modern World

The ancient world had a profound belief in the supernatural. Individual and collective lives were beholden to powers beyond natural comprehension. Respect for the gods was evoked in order that higher powers would intercede favorably rather than judge humans with contempt. In the ancient world, priests, sages, and seers were highly respected because they were perceived to be connected to the world beyond the senses. While the ancient world was deeply spiritual, it was not more morally conscientious—at least not as we may define morality. For example, an ancient inscription north of Ephesus read, "Whoever wishes to visit the temple of the goddess, whether a resident of the city or anyone else, must refrain from intercourse with one's spouse that day, and from intercourse with another other than one's spouse for the preceding two days, and must complete the required ministrations."[2]

The Bible and the Christian church, as we know them, appeared in such a world. The ancient Hebrews insisted there was one true God who alone must be worshiped and whose moral law must be kept. The rest of the ancient world tolerated monotheism but did not fully embrace the concept. Christianity was birthed out of a commitment to the one true God but insisted that this one God in three persons had visited the planet in

---

2. Barr, *New Testament Story*, 108.

human form. This God-man was none other than Jesus of Nazareth, who came to reveal the justice and love of God for the whole world. Christianity was born into a world that, if not more morally exacting, was more superstitious, full of fear and wonder. The pre-modern world view accepted the idea of god(s) and demons but was hesitant to affirm Christianity's belief that God entered this world in human flesh. However, in the Middle Ages, Christianity became a dominant world view. Anselm, Bishop of Canterbury's dictum, "I believe therefore I understand" summarized the thinking of the period."[3] Christians of the pre-modern world believed that all things could be understood through faith. A fitting symbol of that era might have been the clerical or academic robe, suggesting authority and power. By the late fifteenth century, however, the pre-modern view of reality had become suspect and it gradually passed away.

The Modern World

The birth of the modern world is often associated with the Enlightenment of the eighteenth century, but its foundation was laid two hundred years before, during the Renaissance, when human beings were elevated to the center of existence. The prevailing philosophy proposed that modern people, through an appropriate use of reason, could discern the workings of the world. Enlightenment thinkers conceived of the autonomous self, no longer dependent upon gods and spiritual forces to experience the good life. The universe was now seen as an enigma to be solved; therefore, the unknown need no longer be feared. A world of dependable laws and rational principles could be trusted; thus, an optimistic future could be predicted and even expected. The motto of modernity might be, "I believe whatever can be proven."

---

3. Long, *Emerging Hope*, 64.

The Enlightenment was indeed filled with optimism. Enlightenment people believed that if human beings were simply open to empirical truth and discarded superstition, then the good life could be experienced by all. "In the beginning the Enlightenment was an attempt to achieve certainty about God, not an attempt to get rid of God."[4] However, modernity tended to move the belief in God to the margin of society and elevated reason as the god of the new age. Christian leaders realized that the message of the church had to be defended in the language of the new era if it was to have any credibility at all. While the clerical robe might have been an appropriate symbol of the premodern world, the science lab coat was the garb of the modern world.

Postmodern World

If the modern world was optimistic, the postmodern world may be described as pessimistic, or at best suspicious, because the optimistic promises of the modern world did not hold true. With World War I, the grand idea that knowledge could produce utopia and the world could live in peace through shared knowledge proved to be wrong. Bill Kynes noted, "Over and against modernist optimism, a postmodernist mood of irony and playfulness has arisen, expressing a deep seated pessimism. Life is considered to be fragile, threatened by environmental disaster or economic decline."[5]

A theme for the postmodern world might be, "I believe in whatever works for you." Rugged individualism gives way to community found within smaller like-minded groups. Rules are questioned and freedom of expression is encouraged. The best image of postmodernity might be the rock star, who symbolizes self-expression over cultural conformity. While postmodernity is

---

4. Ibid., 65.
5. Kynes, "Postmodernism," 104.

certainly emerging in the Western world, its content is difficult to define. Several postures help to describe, if not define, the emerging cultural reality.

Current Cultural Postures

In the emerging culture, some people still maintain a posture of spirituality; however, this spirituality is not understood as it was in times past. Institutional spirituality is viewed with suspicion, while loyalty to particular denominations or religions is becoming passé. Rules and rituals appear outdated, while individual experiences of spirituality are celebrated.

> *Newsweek* published a double issue with the cover story titled 'Spirituality in America...with convincing research. The *Newsweek* cover story pointed out that nearly 80 percent of Americans under the age of sixty described themselves as "spiritual." Almost two-thirds of them prayed every day and 75 percent of them acknowledged that a very important reason for their faith was to "forge a personal relationship with God." But at the same time, just over a third of Americans attended church weekly.[6]

The emerging culture appears to hold an ingenuous regard for God, even a high regard for Jesus; nonetheless, the church in the Western world is seeing a mass exodus, especially among the young.[7] It would be too simplistic (and in most cases wrong) to conclude that those who have left the church are now atheists. Today, many might describe themselves as believers but not belongers. In this respect, the postmodern world is closer to the

---

6. Lyons, *Next Christians*, 27.
7. Kinnaman, *You Lost Me*, 15.

pre-modern world than the modern world. People are more open to realities beyond the analysis of human reason.

Another postmodern posture prizes diversity over orthodoxy. The idea that "one size fits all" in theological belief or religious practice is neither philosophically nor practically palatable. The modern idea of ecumenical unity (with its assimilation of theological differences) is out while a celebration of diversity is in. However, for good or bad, a celebration of diversity leads to a demand for tolerance. "In a postmodern reading, absolutist claims to reality, or meta-narratives, are nothing but power grabs and conspiracies to legitimize the dominate power structures and to marginalize, trivialize and oppress those whose experiences do not fit."[8]

A respect for diversity assumes that moral right is whatever feels right to me. Truth becomes subject to the opinions of an individual or at least to a small community of friends. Truth claims are questionable because postmoderns believe such assertions may be simply methods of control by those in power. Communication in the emerging culture requires people claiming truth to hold their perception of truth with the glove of humility. "In the modern world the gospel was attacked by those who claimed it was not true. In a postmodern world it is attacked because it claims to be true."[9] Postmodern Christians, while believing there is such a thing as absolute truth, are careful to point out that one may not claim to know the truth in its entirety.

A third postmodern posture gives supreme allegiance to community. Postmodernity has moved from the Renaissance concept of humanism (i.e., the conviction that the individual is the measure of all things) to group think. The modern world placed a high emphasis on the individual. Rugged individualism was

---

8. Kynes, "Postmodernism," 106.
9. Ibid. 107.

affirmed in church and culture. Modern people believed they would prosper when they determined a responsible course of action, worked hard, and did not quit. (In its most extreme manifestations, this kind of individualism hijacked the reality of the church as a community of believers, since biblical faith was always intended to be communal.) But now we have swung to the other end of the pendulum's arc. We believe and do whatever our "tribe" believes and does.

While it is healthy for the emerging culture to rediscover the value of community, some community life in postmodern culture is clannish in nature. It is a kind of community reserved for those who are like minded.[10] However, true Christian community extends itself to all who claim the name of the Lord, not simply those whose preferences are similar.

Implications for Evangelism

These postmodern postures have many implications for effective evangelism. First, we need to handle the truth with humility, not hubris. "Helmut Thielicke, a renowned German theologian and preacher, identified credibility as an operative factor in a communicator's ethos."[11] Therefore, evangelists may lead people to Christ with loving actions more effectively than with convincing arguments.

Second, the gospel may best be communicated in our postmodern culture through groups rather than through solo evangelists. The Celtic model of evangelism implemented by St. Patrick (fifth century) invited believers and nonbelievers into life together.[12] Christian faith was experienced through love

---

10. Long, *Emerging Hope*, 102.
11. Hunter, *Celtic Way of Evangelism*, 59.
12. Ibid., 26.

in action and often became the compelling reason to believe. Celtic evangelism was less individualistic and more communal. In today's postmodern context, where people have become cynical toward Christianity because of the sins of the institutional church, belonging will often precede believing.

Third, evangelism in the emerging postmodern culture may move away from larger stadium events into smaller venues where communication is more conversational. Some larger events may still have a place, but they are likely to take the form of a festival rather than a crusade, camp meeting, or revival service. Large gatherings may still be an effective way to recruit and train people who are sent out on mission during the evangelism event itself. However, postmodern people are more receptive to talking about Jesus Christ in intimate venues rather than a stadium.

For example, the gospel can be effectively shared through local or international service projects, where believers and nonbelievers work together to meet the needs of vulnerable people. Intentional small-group Bible studies in homes, coffee shops, businesses, and churches can extend genuine hospitality to seekers, with times set aside for honest inquiry. Because of the posture of postmoderns, Christian evangelism is becoming more process- and less crisis-oriented. Postmodern people will not respond to evangelism that they perceive as selling a product for an institution, but they often will consider the way of Jesus as modeled through a patient friend.

Chapter Seven

Discovering Christian Responses to Cultural Change

In this book, I use the term *culture* to signify the postures, principles, and practices that we receive from significant others. These received values are part of our social inheritance and are seldom critiqued, simply acted upon as the natural or right way to live our lives. Culture has been likened to the air we breathe: It surrounds us and we need it to live, but we can't see it or analyze in any detailed way how we came to receive it. If our air is toxic, we become more environmentally aware, but we usually take it for granted.

Culture may also be likened to a global positioning system (GPS) that guides us on our highway journeys. Even someone who does not understand GPS technology can follow the prompts of the unknown voice emanating from the device. For the most part, motorists are not interested in understanding the science of GPS as long as they arrive at their intended destinations without getting lost. Culture is like that for many of us. Though we understand little about how it operates, it helps us make sense of our journey.

"Cultural patterns and processes are constantly undergoing change due to the influence of human beings, for humans are always changing themselves and their cultures."[1] With change there is usually a degree of discomfort, for change is often perceived as loss and loss creates grief. This is why churches must learn to navigate cultural change successfully or face the possibility of irrelevance or demise.

---

1. Kraft, *Christianity in Culture*, 114.

Historically, the church has been forced to deal with cultural change. From the church's first-century infancy to its inclusion as the official religion of the Roman Empire to the fall of the Roman Empire to the uncertainty of the Dark Ages to the Great Schism of the Eastern and Western church to the sixteenth-century Reformation and to what some now are calling the Great Emergence, the church has experienced dramatic cultural changes.[2] Church history teaches that cultural change from within and without is inevitable, and possibly is to be embraced. However, throughout the history of Christianity, many believers have been unwilling to acknowledge or accept cultural change. Some have chosen to flee, fight, or finesse their way through cultural change.

The Flight Response

Some Christians see culture as an evil to be avoided. Therefore, they seek to separate church life from demonic secular and worldly religious associations by attempting to live apart from culture. They *flee* from any cultural change because they identify culture as worldly and under control of the evil one.[3]

The flight response certainly has historical precedent. Early Christians found the Judaic and Greco-Roman cultures to be threatening to their new way of life, so many separated themselves into monastic communities as a way to practice holiness and devotion to Christ alone. The flight away from culture was not an attempt to militate against that dominant culture but simply an effort to establish an alternative culture that might be more amenable to Christian values.

Today's Christians in the flight mode have strategically created their own independent denominations, schools, universities,

---

2. Tickle, *Great Emergence*, 16.
3. 1 John 2:15–16; 5:19.

entertainment venues, athletic centers, and then encouraged members to "come out from among them" (2 Cor 6:17) and associate with other like-minded believers, keeping themselves safe from worldly influences. Theologically, the flight-from-culture response sees the world as unredeemable and headed for destruction.

Evangelistic Christians in the flight-from-culture mode have a genuine concern for the purity of the church and for sinners headed for destruction. From a safe distance, these believers warn people to repent of their personal sins and join a Bible-believing community to prepare for the life to come. Positively speaking, these separatist communities provide spiritual security for their members; but an unintended consequence is that outsiders often perceive Christian separatism as an expression of religious superiority.

The Fight Response

Other Christians see culture as something to be transformed. "Culture, therefore, is seen as corrupted but convertible, usable, perhaps even redeemable by God's grace and power. Culture is perverted but not evil in essence."[4] They believe Christians are called to be "salt and light" to make the world a better place. These believers understand the world not solely in negative terms, for the New Testament cautions us to "not love the world" (1 John 2:15) but also reminds us, "God so loved the world" (John 3:16). Culture is not to be surrendered to the evil one. On the contrary, Christians who believe they have a transformative calling feel "under obligation to carry on cultural work in obedience to the Lord."[5]

---

4. Kraft, *Christianity in Culture*, 113.
5. Ibid., 112.

The church militant must *fight* if the cultural war is to be won. In his book *Militant Christians,* George Marsden observes that in the latter part of the twentieth century the old fundamentalism put on the new clothes of the Moral Majority.[6] This movement united some white evangelicals, African American Christians, Catholics, Jews, Mormons, and political conservatives of no particular religious persuasion as militant comrades. They came together as a result of their distress over cultural changes that they saw taking place. Passive church members came out of their separatist conclaves to counter the exclusion of public prayer and the inclusion of biological evolution in public schools. Militant Christians on the Right decried the negative impacts of women's rights, pornography, homosexuality, and humanism. They also expressed concern for the loss of a belief in American exceptionalism. Strategically, conservative Christians engaged culture by running for public office, hosting radio and television talk shows, publishing books and videos—strategies advocating a return to the Judeo-Christian values they believed were endangered.

Liberal Christians and religiously unaffiliated leaders of secular culture did not surrender the fight, however. Through political activism, they aggressively advocated for same-sex marriage, abortion rights, freedom of artistic expression, the ordination of gay and lesbian clergy, and the denunciation of American colonialism.

Both conservative and liberal militant Christians wedded the gospel to American politics. Rightly or wrongly, they comingled their faith with viral political rhetoric. Major political parties hoped to take advantage of this, co-opting Jesus' message in ways that left some folks rejecting both political and religious activism. War always leaves casualties. When the response to cultural change is to fight, we often see unintended consequences for both church and culture.

---

6. Marsden, *Militant Christians,* 83.

The Finesse Response

Some Christians understand culture to be neutral, neither something to flee or fight. As Charles Kraft puts it, "Culture is not in and of itself either an enemy or friend of God or humans. It is, rather, something that is there to be used by personal beings such as humans, God, and Satan."[7] We might call this approach Christianity's *finesse* response to culture. In other words, it is the effort to affirm culture for what it is and to believe that God often uses cultural change to bring about spiritual renewal.

Christians who hold this view see the emerging culture as an evangelistic opportunity. Instead of seeing cultural change as evil, they seek to influence that change through active engagement with it. These Christians speak prophetically within the church, encouraging believers to bring both good news and good works to their surrounding communities. They attempt to interact with those outside the Christian community through dialogue rather than debate. They prefer to embody an apologetic of God's love and grace rather than engage in confrontational evangelism based only on propositional truths.

These culture-competent Christians possess a renewed commitment to the kingdom of God lived out in the context of neighborhoods, cities, states, and world. They invite people to experience the good news through authentic relationships with those who love Jesus. As friends and neighbors observe genuine Christian community in action, they will be drawn in by agape love as opposed to logical arguments.

Gabe Lyons, in his book *The Next Christians,* suggests that Christians need to participate in culture by pronouncing that all of life is divine vocation and no region of culture is beyond redemption. He observes that Jesus entered into life with all kinds of people and determined to create communities of reconciliation

---

7. Kraft, *Christianity in Culture*, 113.

and restoration with them. [8] Lyons identifies seven channels of cultural influence, reminding us that "brokenness exists within each channel of culture."[9] If Christians are to be culturally competent, they must find intentional ways to enter media, arts, entertainment, government, church, education, business to simply be the people of God. While these culture-competent Christians may not evangelize in traditional ways, they believe the integrity of their lives and lips will communicate authentically to a watching world.

In summary, these descriptions of Christian responses to culture are based on their varying beliefs about culture. Believers' views of the world will guide their evangelistic strategy. Whether we believe the surrounding culture is something to evade, exchange, or engage will determine our approaches for effective evangelism. The important question is, Are disciples being made? If not, then our evangelistic strategies ought to be challenged.

---

8. Lyons, *Next Christians*, 116.
9. Ibid., 117.

Chapter Eight

Deploying Diversely Gifted Disciples

"But you will receive power when the Holy Spirit comes on you; and you will be my witnesses in Jerusalem, and in all Judea and Samaria, and to the ends of the earth" (Acts 1:8).

Jesus instructed his disciples to tarry in Jerusalem until the promised gift of the Holy Spirit should come. He explained that it was best that he go away so that the Comforter would come to gift and guide his disciples. The disciples had their doubts, but they knew one thing for sure: They were not ready to do anything on their own. Disillusioned, discouraged, and depressed, they waited for comfort and empowerment to do what Jesus commissioned them to do. As Jesus ascended to the Father, he had said, "You will receive power...you will be my witnesses." Significantly, his words were not directed to "you" the individual (second person singular), but rather to "you" the group (second person plural). Also note that the verb translated "will be" is in the "declarative form rather than the imperative, meaning witnessing is a natural assumed part of the disciples' life-style not simply a planned activity or event."[1]

The first evangelists were the diversely gifted women and men Jesus called to be with him while he ministered here on earth. As Jesus began his earthly ministry, he appointed Twelve that "they might be with him and that he might send them out to preach" (Mark 3:14). These men became known as the Apostles, a term that simply meant "those sent forth." From the beginning of his

---

1. Arn and Arn, *Master's Plan for Making Disciples*, 20.

ministry, Jesus prepared the Twelve to be sent out to share the good news with all who would listen (Luke 9:1–6). Their "sending out" did not begin with his ascension, but long before that.

However, with the ascension, Jesus commissioned all of his followers—not just the Twelve—to go into the entire world and preach the gospel. As recipients of the Great Commission, both women and men were to become apostles in the sense that all believers were sent forth to share good news.[2] Thus, the church is often called the "apostolic community."

In addition to Apostles, the early church appointed bishops, presbyters, and deacons to engage in the ministry of evangelism. Their ministries were more localized as they gave oversight to the life and work of local assemblies. However, even these local overseers were to teach the faith and maintain a personal character that would be compelling to those outside the Christian community (1 Tim 3:1–7).

Another group of evangelists often overlooked in the early history of the church were theologians and philosophers. Theologians started schools that taught converts the way of Christ and attempted to answer the critics of Christianity, a ministry known as *apologetics*.[3] The church's early theologians believed that followers of the Way should not be ignorant, even though they were "fools for Christ" (1 Cor 4:10).

Apostles, presbyters, bishops, deacons, theologians, and philosophers—all were full-time evangelists in the sense that they were preaching, teaching, and witnessing to the truth of Christ, both formally and informally. However, these full-time evangelistic workers were not the only ones spreading the gospel.

---

2. Wijngaards, *Ordination of Women in the Catholic Church*, 134–35. The author presents evidence of women's involvement in every aspect of leadership in the church for nine centuries until squelched by the dominating Latin culture.

3. Green, *Evangelism in the Early Church*, 171. Early philosophers were Pantaenus, missionary to India; Justin in Rome; and Origen in Alexandria.

Historian Adolf von Harnack was on target when he declared, "It is impossible to see any one class of people inside the church as chief agents of the Christian propaganda. On the contrary, we cannot hesitate to believe that the great ministry of Christianity was in reality accomplished by means of informal missionaries."[4]

Indeed, it is difficult to identify any one group in the early church as being responsible for the evangelistic enterprise, because for more than two hundred years, there was no formal distinction between clergy and laity. Laity (*layos*) in the early church simply meant "the people of God," while clergy (*kleros*) were people "called out to follow Christ." The only difference was that some traveled and did gospel ministry full time, while others remained in local communities to work and serve. Not until the end of the second century was a line drawn between the duties of clergy and laity.[5] By the third century, that line of demarcation became a great chasm.

With the division of duties between clergy and laity, a religious class system developed. Clergy were accorded higher status. In the third century, clergy assumed a more dominant role in ecclesiastical leadership and the laity was relegated to a more compliant role in church life and witness. Thus, evangelization was assumed to be the work of professionals. Much later, the Protestant Reformation tried to bridge the chasm by asserting the priesthood of all believers (1 Peter 2:9); however, even during the Reformation, this was more rhetoric than reality.

Today, as in the early church, evangelism is most effective when it is understood to be the call and task of all the people of God. Robert Coleman asserts, "There are only three references in the New Testament to those who are evangelists (with the special gift of evangelism) but Scripture contains over 120 references to

---

4. Ibid, 172.
5. Faivre and Smith, *Emergence of the Laity*, 7–15.

the broader commission to all members of the Church to preach the Gospel and make disciples."[6] Church history reveals that evangelism has been least effective when relegated to a gifted few. By contrast, the New Testament records that early Christians witnessed to the claims of Christ everywhere they went—and thousands responded.

Loren Mead insists the church of the twenty-first century is no longer part of a Christian-dominated culture. In many ways, we can expect to face opposition similar to that of the first century. Mead points out, "The early church consisted of faithful Christians huddling together (congregating) for worship, prayer and mutual support amid a hostile and antagonistic external environment. The mission field was right outside the door." Mead calls this situation "the Apostolic Paradigm."[7]

Such is the context for evangelization in the newly emerging culture. If the church of the twenty-first century is to recover its nerve for evangelism, then it must move away from clerical professionalism toward evangelism as a way of life for all Christians.

Christian Witness

Your personal Christian witness is linked directly to your evangelism work. Properly understood, your Christian witness is who you are, more than what you do. To be an effective witness depends on your abilities and activities only to a limited extent, but it has everything to do with your credibility. Pastor Heather Kirk-Davidoff writes, "A good witness tells the truth and has the perceived credibility to back it up."[8] She polled a group of attorneys and judges to

---

6. Coleman, *Mind of the Master*, 9.
7. As quoted in Diehl, *Ministry in Daily Life*, 5–6.
8. As quoted in Johnson, *Got Style?*, 2.

discover what they considered good qualities of a credible witness. The following is a summary of her discoveries:

1. Good witnesses look the decision maker (judge or jury) in the eyes when answering a question.
2. Good witnesses speak in a confident manner—they don't hesitate or stumble over their words.
3. Good witnesses listen carefully to the questions they are asked.
4. Good witnesses answer the questions they are asked directly and stop talking when they've given their answers.
5. Good witnesses speak in plain language that every listener can understand.
6. Good witnesses do not argue when questioned.
7. Good witnesses if they do not know the answer to a question say so. [9]

Good witnesses are people of character who speak when opportunities are presented, who listen because they genuinely care about people, and who act as humble servants to those in their sphere of influence.

Empowering Witnesses in Daily Life

Pastoral leadership in the emerging culture must empower the whole church to share the good news in natural ways, within daily contexts of activity. When speaking to a graduating class of ministers and missionaries, E. Stanley Jones is reported to have said, "Your future ministry will either be a field or a force." Dr. Jones implied that ministry could be a field where the graduates would go

---

9. Ibid.

to preach, pray, counsel, and serve, or it could be a force by which they would help people in their local congregations to discover their God-given call and equip them to use those gifts for kingdom work. Clearly, congregational leaders will influence more people for Christ if they see their ministry as more than a field of personal activity in their community. Their outreach grows exponentially when they help other believers become credible employers, employees, parents, citizens, and church members.

The Work Place

On average, an American adult will work 100,000 hours in a lifetime.[10] However, most Christians do not see their workplace as a mission field. Listen to the lament of one businessman:

> In the almost 30 years of my professional career, my church has never once suggested that there be any type of accounting of my on-the-job ministry to others...There has never been an inquiry into the types of ethical decisions I must face, or whether I seek to communicate the faith to my co-workers. I have never been in a congregation where there was any type of public affirmation of a ministry in my career (as a sales manager). In short, I must conclude that my church really doesn't have the least interest in whether or how I minister in my daily work.[11]

The workplace is a most effective place for Christian witness. In the workplace, through natural conversations, co-workers routinely disclose their passions, pains, and problems. Credible witnesses listen and respond in ways that are Christlike. If they are

---

10. Armstrong, "The Other 100,000 Hours," 20.
11. Ibid., 21

to train others for effective evangelistic work, ordained ministers need to close the gap that often exists between themselves and the working people in their pews. Here are some suggestions for doing that:

- Be present in the work sphere and listen carefully.
- Become workplace literate (for example, by reading the *Wall Street Journal*).
- Preach to work concerns.
- Use adult education, small groups, and retreats to address workers' sense of work-faith disjunction.
- Train laity in devotional disciplines linked to their work and daily lives.[12]

The Community

Many church members are active citizens in their communities. They are already involved in service clubs, public and private schools, health clubs, Little League sports, the arts, and political organizations. Pastors must help their people realize they are points of light wherever they go. In their communities, they can expose moral and spiritual darkness and engage in incarnational evangelism. Effective Christian witnesses discover places where God's light is already shining in the darkness so they can call attention to it and support Christ-honoring activity wherever it is found.

The Home

Most hours of the week are spent in the home. Whether single or married, everyone has a place they call home, but traditional

---

12. Ibid.

home life is changing. A family consisting of a female and male married couple with two children and a pet is no longer the norm. More and more, the home is a place of blended families that result from divorce and remarriage, custodial families in which grandparents raise their grandchildren, and so on. The home is another mission field where members of your congregation are already serving. The church needs to help families pass down the faith from generation to generation in their homes.[13] Families progress through lifecycles, so congregational leaders must equip family leaders in ways to build faith in each season of life. Skill development for single and married parents, budget management, marriage enrichment, divorce recovery, retirement planning, time and stress management—all of these can prepare people to share the gospel within their families. Members of households need to be reminded that the home is a legitimate place for Christian witness.

The Congregation

The local congregation is the place where Christians gather for two to three hours a week to worship God, support each other emotionally and spiritually, and receive training to go back out into the mission field. Healthy congregations continue to be the most effective means to empower Christians to become effective witnesses. As we saw in our earlier discussion of incorporational evangelism, both qualitative and quantitative spiritual growth takes place when there is a healthy interplay of teaching, fellowship, and service. Research in healthy church development identifies these eight characteristics that are necessary if church health is to be sustained:

---

13. For more on this subject, see Stephenson, *Smooth Hand Offs*, and Adcock, *Call to Grandparenting*.

- Empowering leadership: giving people permission to follow their passion.
- Gift-oriented ministry: helping people to discover their spiritual gifts.[14]
- Passionate spirituality: encouraging people to discover a life of devotion.
- Functional structures: removing barriers that restrict personal and corporate growth.
- Inspiring worship: discovering ways to draw people close to God.
- Holistic small groups: creating environments where people can know and be known.
- Need-oriented evangelism: finding needs and filling them.
- Loving relationships: expressing radical grace to all people.[15]

This research emphasizes that "no church wanting to grow qualitatively and quantitatively can afford to overlook any of these eight quality characteristics."[16] Healthy, growing churches, are being continually renewed through the guiding presence of the Holy Spirit so that their mission continues from generation to generation. Congregations committed to equipping their people to be effective Christian witnesses in daily life will move from tightly controlled organizations where clergy do all the ministry to an environment in which spiritually gifted members know they are called and capable to do ministry, both inside and outside of traditional church activities.

---

14. See appendix 1 for a spiritual gifts assessment.
15. Schwarz, *Natural Church Development*, 16–37.
16. Ibid., 38.

Witnessing in Daily Life Case Study

Two congregations in the Eastern United States determined they were going to change their ministry paradigms from clergy-centered ministry to lay-centered ministry. One congregation implemented this change by reorganizing their system of church governance. The other did it by using their traditional governance structure. Their experience suggests that there is no one-size-fits-all congregational structure to deploy diversely gifted disciples.[17]

While the two congregations are organized differently, both affirm there is no qualitative difference between clergy and laity. In fact, one congregation chose to do away with the term *lay* or *layperson* because those terms might suggest some people were less than ministers. Both congregations emphasize the fact that all believers, whether ordained or non-ordained, have a daily ministry or mission to fulfill. They focus their effort in three areas:

1. Members *affirmed* for their ministries
2. Members *equipped* to carry out their ministries
3. Members *supported* in various ways by congregational leaders.

Affirmation Ministries

Preaching can affirm the importance of ministry in daily life—through sermon illustrations, for example. Such preaching may be aided by focus groups in which members share daily life issues. These two affirming congregations periodically engage their people in worship leadership, not only those who routinely work within the four walls of the church but also those engaged in workplace ministries. When congregational members who do most of their ministry in daily life are also utilized in public worship, they can use their other spiritual gifts.

---

17. Diehl, *Ministry in Daily Life*, 12.

These two congregations use special days, such as Labor Day, to affirm ministry and mission in daily life. They use newsletters, websites, banners, bulletins, and banquets to bring awareness to the significant Christian witness that their people share in their communities.

Equipping Ministries

Sunday and weekday congregational gatherings can be good times to equip people for service. One congregation developed "The Center for Faith and Life," which offered four-week courses dealing with the ministry areas of occupation, family, community, and church. Some of the courses offered were

- How to Manage Controversy
- Work and Family
- His, Hers, and Ours (children)
- Christian Ethics and Business
- Ministry in Health Care
- Christians with Public Responsibility
- Environmental Stewardship
- CPR Course
- Christians and the Constitution
- Financial Planning
- Christian Doctrine
- Lenten Series
- Evangelizing without Turning People Off[18]

Support Ministries

Ministry and mission in daily life can be emotionally draining. Every believer needs personal support for ministry, whether serving in

---

18. Ibid., 36.

the secular workplace, home, community, or official church activities. Congregational small groups are often task-oriented because ministry must be accomplished, but these two congregations resolved to gather their people to be strengthened for the journey. They offered the following support groups to those engaged in ministry:

- Shepherd zones by Zip Code providing pastoral care
- Intergenerational fellowship groups providing fun and laughter
- Women's groups
- Men's groups
- Youth groups
- Retirement groups
- Discernment groups
- Prayer groups
- Accountability groups[19]

Evangelism in the twenty-first century requires a paradigm shift in which the old command-and-control hierarchies of modernity give way to collaborative models of leadership. Congregations who survive and thrive will become apostolic sending stations in a somewhat hostile culture. In spite of that resistance, Christians must recover their nerve and go into their respective worlds with the gospel. Fewer people will rush to our congregations because church membership is a cultural norm. On the contrary, an antagonistic culture may seek to thwart the work of the church. Even so, Christ must be shared in word and deed in the workplace, community, home, and even with nominal Christians inside the walls of the church.

---

19. Ibid., 52–60.

Chapter Nine

Developing Effective Evangelistic Strategies

As we all know, a *strategy* is a plan to help an organization accomplish its mission. In many ways, Christian evangelism is synonymous with strategy: How do we connect God's salvific work with human needs? Over the centuries, the church has seen periods of growth and decline, and church attendance in America is currently in decline. But we dare not shrug that off as a normal cyclical occurrence. While church attendance is not the only marker of whether evangelization is taking place, declining church attendance has been a leading indicator of waning evangelism efforts. Today, "only 41 percent of Americans attend church services on a typical weekend. Each new generation becomes increasingly unchurched."[1]

Table 1: Who Attends Church in America Each Weekend?

Generation	Birth Years	Percentage Attending Church
Builders	Before 1946	51%
Boomers	1946–1964	41%
Busters	1965–1976	34%
Bridgers	1977–1994	29%

In comparison with Western Europe, these American percentages are quite high; nonetheless, the number of people attending church in the West is on a downward trajectory. (Some

---

1. Rainer, *Surprising Insights from the Unchurched*, 33.

feel that American church statistics may be exaggerated since they are based on telephone surveys and therefore subject to the so-called "hallo effect"—i.e., people expressing their intentions rather than their actual practice.[2] These critics estimate real weekend church attendance may be closer to 20 percent of the American population.)

Many factors account for the decline in church attendance and membership. Frankly, one major reason is the church has lost its first love (Rev 2:4). Seldom do people find a contagious spirituality that attracts them. Ninety percent of churches in the United States have not baptized a single convert in the past year.[3] Evangelism flows out of a love for God and a desire that lost people are found. We face great danger when congregations become accustomed to "business as usual" without conversions, baptisms, or congregational multiplication. Such congregations rarely close their doors, but their missional impact is limited and pride becomes the only reason for their continued existence.

Another cause for decline, especially among the young, is a watered-down version of the gospel that demands little of them. Kenda Creasy Dean, a Methodist pastor and Princeton Theological Seminary faculty member, points the finger at adults who have failed to challenge youth to a costly discipleship. According to Dean, a costly discipleship has been replaced by a "moralistic-therapeutic-deism."[4] Young people are encouraged to be good, have positive self-esteem, and believe in a God who is nonjudgmental, available whenever you need supernatural help, and ready to welcome all people to heaven when they die. This low-cost discipleship has not captivated the hearts

2. Gibbs and Bolger, Emerging Churches, 19.

3. Jon Baker, conversation with the author at Pastors Roundtable, Henderson, Nevada, February 2013.

4. Dean, Almost Christian, 14.

and minds of young people, so they have simply checked out of church.[5]

Another reason the church is witnessing an exodus is because of a credibility crisis. The scandal of clergy abuse, ecclesiastical financial irresponsibility, and old patriarchal leadership that ignores gifted women leaders, accompanied by cronyism and unexamined traditionalism, has created disgust among many Americans. They have tried institutional Christianity and found it wanting. Some reject God altogether and turn to atheism or agnosticism. Still others choose to practice Christianity outside the institutional church. This is why some church leaders say that Americans now live in a post-Christian society.

Another reason for decline is more theologically based because people of the twenty-first century have begun to question whether a person needs to come to Christ for salvation. They see world religions in a more positive light, as agencies of salvation. The concept of universal salvation, while not new, is experiencing a revival. In the minds of many, Paul's passing comment that some who have never heard the gospel might still be saved (cf. Rom. 15:21) justifies the belief that all people probably will be saved. So they feel less urgency to share the gospel with others.

In his book *Will Many Be Saved?,* Ralph Martin acknowledges the possibility that those who have never heard the gospel may be saved, providing they live up to what has been revealed in their inner conscience. However, Martin goes on to point out that often these conditions for salvation are not met. As a result, the theologians of Vatican II concluded that "the salvation of non-Christians who do not meet these conditions is significantly tied

---

5. Fortunately, Dean can point to several discipleship models that are transferring faith to the new generation. See Dean, *Almost Christian*, for further details.

to the gospel being effectively preached to them."[6] We cannot assume that a salvific possibility is a universal probability, thus releasing us from Christ's call to evangelize.

We need to confront such negative trends honestly. We need to seek the guidance of the Holt Spirit for renewal of our gospel mission, because only God can renew congregations through the power of the Holy Spirit. Clearly, it is God's will that we make disciples and teach Christ's Word to all people. The Holy Spirit is still drawing women and men to Christ, so it is incumbent upon church leaders to remove any obstacles that impede evangelistic growth.

Holy Discernment

Strategic planning to extend the community of faith requires an ongoing holy conversation between believers, related to intentional evangelism at home and abroad. The important thing is not whether a local congregation has a written strategic plan for evangelism, but whether the church has reflected seriously on its mission and whether it is fulfilling that mission. Rendle and Mann write, "Planning is a structured conversation about what a group of people believe God calls them to be or do."[7] Leaders with responsibility for the ministry of evangelism must periodically invite other believers to consider three questions:

1. Who are we?
2. What has God called us to do?
3. Who is our neighbor?[8]

---

6. Martin, *Will Many Be Saved?*, 58.
7. Rendle and Mann, *Holy Conversations*, 3.
8. Ibid., 5.

1. Who Are We?

Strategic planning as a spiritual practice begins with the question, "Who are we as a congregation?" This first question includes, but goes beyond, an assessment of the local congregation's denominational or movemental affiliation. The question has to do with the congregation's identity as the people of God. While the local church is part of the universal church, the universal church is represented in a localized way. There is always a creative tension between the church up close and personal and the church universal and historical. The universal church has a long history, and the contemporary situation requires that we understand its historical roots as well as its contemporary expression.

Howard Snyder argues that the local church "should be structured on spiritual gifts of leadership and on some form of large-group and small group gatherings. Beyond this, the church should take care to distinguish between its essential self and all para-church structures so it does not become culture-bound, and so that, conversely, in periods of upheaval the wine is not thrown out with the wineskins."[9]

Since a local church comprises Spirit-gifted people of God who gather together in groups both large and small, it is cross-cultural in nature. The church must remain true to its organizational core, but flexible in its non-essential identity, in order to be culturally relevant in each generation. Each local representation of the church has a unique identity that has developed out of its cultural context, and this identity may be quite different (with regard to tradition, style, and doctrine) from any other congregation down the street or across town. While this local identity is important, it is not the essence of the congregation's purpose.

A holy conversation about evangelism should include a discussion about missional aspects of the local church's identity

---

9. Snyder, *Problem of Wineskins*, 165.

that are essential and cross-cultural, versus characteristics that are provincial and transitory. For example, some congregations affirm the value of women and men as equal partners in ministry, while others restrict leadership opportunities based on gender. It is important for churches to understand and respect their traditions, even if those patterns do not fully express their current convictions about their role in the kingdom. This holy conversation may identify several things that a local assembly cherishes as important and desires to maintain, even though these values may not be embraced by believers in neighboring congregations. If this dialogue can share such matters of local importance with the wider church community, these distinctive values could bring understanding and greater health to the church at large. For example, suppose a local congregation believes that Christian unity is an important but neglected value in its community. If that church models effective ways to demonstrate reconciliation and unity, then the church at large can be informed and strengthened.

Holy conversations also enable congregations to understand that they share many things in common with other institutions. If they are open, congregations can learn a great deal from other organizations, both sacred and secular. We should be willing to learn about the best organizational practices, no matter where they are found. Missiologist George Hunter gives the following examples of things which the church has in common with other organizations:

- All institutions have a mission.
- Institutions both sacred and secular are structured to accomplish their mission.
- All institutions formally or informally resource the mission.
- All institutions cultivate leaders to advance the mission.

- All institutions, through personal conversations, print publications and electronic media, seek to keep members informed about their mission.
- All financially reputable organizations conduct audits to insure the mission is fiscally sound.[10]

A congregation's holy conversation will also discover that Christian churches are distinct from other organizations in several important ways. Hunter lists these factors that make the church a unique kind of organization:

- The church has a distinct source. Christ built it, on the rock of faith in him as Messiah and risen Lord, to be the new Israel, the Body of Christ, and the extension of his incarnation.
- The Church has a distinct message. From the ancient apostles the message of the church is the gospel of the Kingdom of God.
- The church has a distinct purpose—to reach and serve the peoples of the earth, to help them become reconciled to God, liberated from sin, restored to God's purpose, and deployed in God's wider mission seeking health, peace, justice, and salvation for all people and creation.
- The church has a distinct ethic. Through such sources as the Ten Commandments, the Sermon on the Mount, and the Great Commandment to love God and neighbor, the church is given the ethic that should limit, shape, and focus how Christians do Kingdom work.
- The church has a distinct power. As no one can say "Jesus is Lord" except by the Holy Spirit (1 Cor. 12:3), not much else that is supremely important in our total

---

10. Hunter, *Leading and Managing a Growing Church*, 22.

mission is likely to succeed without that third Person's power behind, attending, and blessing our efforts.[11]

Each local congregation should articulate and celebrate its unique identity based on its tradition, doctrine, and ethos. Through this intentional and recurring holy conversation, the congregation affirms its identity by solidifying its core values so as not to be "tossed back and forth by the waves, and blown here and there by every wind of teaching" (Eph 4:14).

2. What Has God Called Us to Do?

In regard to evangelism, this conversation can lead to answering an essential question: "Based on what we know about ourselves and our situation, what do we believe we are to do? How are we to develop or mature?"[12] Many imperatives in Scripture declare what followers of Jesus should do or stop doing. However, according to C. Peter Wagner, none stands out more clearly than the Great Commission (Matt 28:19–20). Wagner unfolds the meaning of the Great Commission by reminding us,

> Of the four action verbs in this statement of the Great Commission, there are three participles while only one is imperative. The imperative, *matheteusate* (make disciples) is clearly the goal of the Great Commission. The participles describe three means which will aid in accomplishing that goal: *poreuthentes* (going), *baptizontes* (baptizing), and *disaskontes* (teaching). Like preaching and witnessing (which Matthew also mentions in 24:14 and 26:13), these activities are essential parts of God's program but never the end in themselves. They all

---

11. Ibid.
12. Rendle and Mann, *Holy Conversations*, 4.

should be used as a part of the process of making disciples. Preaching is a presoteric (before salvation) activity and teaching is a postsoteric (after salvation activity). All are involved in the cyclic process of making disciples.[13]

A holy conversation about the mission of the church must embrace the fact that the church is called to make disciples. Among the many good and biblical things we are called to do, can we point to individuals by name who are now disciples, but who were not disciples last month or last year? Charles Arn forcefully reminds those charged with church leadership of the following mandate:

The bottom line following evangelistic efforts is—does the church grow? Most mass and local church evangelism approaches today have a significant common shortcoming. Attention is centered, and success judged around the goal of getting a decision. This decision-making mentality may actually be one of the reasons national church membership continues to decline, in relation to population growth, in spite of so much being said and done in mass evangelism, media evangelism, evangelism training, and evangelism conferences.[14]

The discipling ministry of the church expresses its commitment to multiplication, not simply addition. Keith Phillips reminds us that "a person truly committed to discipleship will accomplish much more for the Kingdom than an aggressive evangelist."[15] Phillips goes on to mathematically dramatize the effect of those committed to discipling "reliable people who will also be qualified to teach others as well" (2 Tim 2:2).

---

13. Wagner, *Frontiers in Missionary Strategy*, 22.
14. Arn & Arn, *Master's Plan for Making Disciples*, 9–10.
15. Phillips, *Making of a Disciple*, 23.

Table 2: A comparison of Discipleship and Evangelism[16]

Note: Assumes evangelist reaches one person a day, and discipler trains one person a year.

Year	Evangelist	Discipler
1	365	2
2	730	4
3	1095	8
4	1460	16
5	1825	32
6	2190	64
7	2555	128
8	2920	256
9	3285	512
10	3650	1024
11	4015	2048
12	4380	4096
13	4745	8192
14	5110	16,384
15	5475	32,768
16	5840	65,536
17	6205	131,072
18	6570	262,144
19	6935	524,288
20	7300	1,048,576
21	7665	2,097,152
22	8030	4,194,304
23	8395	8,388,608
24	8760	16,777,216
25	9125	33,554,432
26	9490	67,108,864
27	9855	134,217,728
28	10,220	268,435,456
29	10,585	536,870,912
30	10,950	1,073,741,824
31	11,315	2,147,483,648
32	11,680	4,294,967,296

16. Ibid.

Recovering Our Nerve

Congregations must not only multiply disciples but also multiply congregations. Congregations grow in several ways. There is interior, exterior, and expansion growth.

- *Interior* growth takes place when belongers become believers.
- *Exterior* growth transpires when congregations reach out to family, friends and associates and they also become disciples.
- *Expansion* growth takes place when congregations start new congregations which honor native language and cultural differences. [17]

An evangelistically minded church, whether large or small, may concomitantly be involved in the ministry of multiplication. "In God's creation, all living things have been designed to multiply."[18] Therefore, the church must seek to create environments suitable for reproducing believers.

Church Multiplication Case Study

One Southwestern congregation experienced a ten-year gradual decline from 600 to 365 in average Sunday morning attendance. The congregation secured a church consultant to help them assess their situation and develop a growth strategy for the future. The church council believed that external eyes might better discern why the congregation was in a gradual decline.

The consultant, through careful research, discovered that at one time the congregation was the largest church in its

---

17. DeYoung, Emerson, Yancey, and Kim, *United by Faith*, 74. Only 5.5 percent of congregations in the United States are multiracial. DeYoung advocates racially defined churches only when language is a barrier.

18. Schwarz, *Color Your World*, 94.

denomination west of the Mississippi. The congregation had an attraction model of ministry based on solid preaching, dynamic multigenerational music programs, and excellent recreational and youth ministries. The church made a missional commitment to plant another church after the mother church reached a Sunday attendance of one thousand. However, the church never reached the one thousand attendance goal.

The church's property was located in the inner city, an area which had experienced a decade of decline. The local high school had been closed and several neighborhoods razed to make way for a new interstate highway. Many of the congregation's members had relocated to the suburbs, so the congregation had become a drive-in church on weekends.

The consultant worked with a long-range planning committee to discover the best location for the church's future. After a year of prayerful discernment, the following options were considered:

1. Stay put and change the congregation's philosophy of ministry to engage the changing community.
2. Relocation. While this option would deliver the greatest "shock" to the system early on, it might prove to be the best option for evangelistic growth.
3. Develop a satellite location that would test the ministry possibilities there before actually relocating.

The decision was a difficult one, but the congregation elected to adopt portions of options two and three. They began a satellite campus and determined to wait and see what might transpire for the inner-city location. After a year of meeting as one church in two locations, the congregation received a cash offer for its inner-city facility from the local Christian mission, which was being displaced by urban development. By an 80 percent affirmative vote, the congregation decided to relocate to the northwest part of the city, where most of their current members lived. Ten acres of land were donated for facility construction. At the same time, the congregation opted to start another church on the west side of the city, with sixty of their members becoming the core group of the church plant.

One year after the relocation and the new church plant, both churches accounted for 461 weekend worshipers—an increase of 21 percent over the 365 who worshiped together the previous year. Over the next twenty years, two more congregations to the south and east were planted by the mother church. Through this commitment to church multiplication, the 365 average attendance of the "mother congregation" became a combined attendance of 3,372 for the four congregations. Only after the mother church became involved in church planting did it exceed its weekend attendance goal of one thousand.

Missiologist Peter Wagner has said that church planting is the most effective method of evangelism under the sun. Congregations do not have to be megachurches to think about church multiplication. In their strategic planning, all congregations can actively pursue church planting. After all, the mission of the universal church is to make disciples and multiply churches.

3. Who Is Our Neighbor?

The third question related to strategic evangelism planning has to do with identifying those people who are not yet part of the community of faith. Over the course of church history, Christians have used several terms to describe people who are not part of a local congregation. In ancient times, the word *pagan* designated those who were not part of the Christian community. In more recent years, the terms *unchurched* or *prechurched* have become common designations. Futurist Leonard Sweet thinks such terminology is dated and recommends calling the people beyond the door of the church simply "ordinary people."

James Nieman and Thomas Rogers suggest *neighbor* as a more suitable way to talk about people who are not yet part of a local congregation. Rogers and Nieman believe *neighbor* is a warm and inviting word, whereas terms such as *unchurched* have negative connotations. If effective evangelism is the goal, then we must use care in selecting the words we use to identify people beyond the local assembly. Neiman and Rogers remind us that

> *neighbors'* Greek root alludes to location, one who is nearby. Moreover, this New Testament usage assumes an underlying Hebrew concept emphasizing relationship. The neighbor is someone we regularly meet, a fellow participant in social encounters. At the same time, however, the neighbor is clearly not a member of the household.[19]

There are many informal ways we get to know our neighbors. Some we get to know by walking around the block, others while shopping at the grocery store, still others while working out at health clubs or attending sporting events. Some neighbors we know by name, others only by face. We know something about neighbors by the houses they own or apartments they rent, clothes they wear, and company they keep. Some neighbors we encounter frequently and others only occasionally.

Another more formal way to intentionally discover neighbors is to begin a friendly fact-finding study of surrounding neighborhoods. Using this approach, selected members will walk the streets and make observations regarding the community. Are there single-family homes or apartment buildings here? Are the streets and sidewalks in good repair? Are there schools or retirement communities in the neighborhood? Such a visual survey begins to identify our ministry context.

---

19. Nieman and Rogers, *Preaching to Every Pew*, 13.

A more scientific approach is to use the resources of the Percept organization.[20] Many denominational planning offices and local congregations use this data-gathering organization to determine current and future population growth, ethnicity make-up, receptivity to faith, social concerns, and desired communication patterns.[21] Such information allows congregations to be culturally sensitive to the hopes, dreams, fears, and aspirations of neighbors. When a congregation's leaders are aware of the real and felt needs of a community, they can design ministries that connect with the community rather than simply experiment with the good intentions or favorite ministries of a few people.

After local leaders have engaged in intentional holy conversation and thoroughly investigated the three strategic questions about congregational identity, mission, and context, then they are ready to develop an evangelism strategy. Leaders must ask, in light of this preparation, "How are we going to accomplish our mission? Where and when will we begin?" While the mission to make disciples is universal, congregational efforts to reach particular communities will differ. As we have seen, congregations differ from one another, and those differences will enable evangelism to take place in culturally compatible ways.

Midwestern Case Study

One Midwestern congregation discovered itself in an unexpected period of decline, so their leadership team went into a season of discernment regarding its past, present, and future. These leaders realized that they needed to do more than tweak the existing ministry plan. They entered into a strategic planning process, which the church council determined would take twelve to eighteen

---

20. Rendle and Mann, *Holy Conversations*, 276–77.
21. See appendix 2 for an example of a Percept report.

months. Because "the congregation was clearly out of sync with the location and time, the congregation must become more strategic in its planning."[22] They undertook a SWOT analysis to discover the strengths, weaknesses, opportunities, and threats that faced them, since these internal and external conditions would influence congregational change over time.[23] Through their SWOT analysis, the congregation discovered the following:

Strengths

For fifteen years, the congregation had experienced exceptional growth and was one of the ten largest churches its denomination. The church had equipped its members to be involved in personal evangelism. At the same time, their discipleship programs flourished and the church was involved in local and international missionary efforts.

Because of the congregation's commitment to evangelism, it outgrew its facility. At great expense, the congregation relocated to a property on the outskirts of town in an expected growth corridor to expand its ministry base. In the second year of this relocation effort, the church reached its largest weekly attendance of 1,583 in Sunday worship. Even though finances were tight, the congregation continued to flourish.

Weaknesses

In the third year after their relocation, the local and national economy went into decline. At the same time, the congregation made a controversial change in pastoral leadership. As a result, their financial giving declined and the church came close to defaulting on its mortgage. The state cancelled plans to build a major roadway, which had been a strategic reason for choosing the church's

---

22. Rendle and Mann, *Holy Conversations*, 11.
23. Ibid., 18–29.

new location. Worship attendance and financial support fell to half of their previous levels, but fixed expenses remained the same. There was a sense of discouragement.

Opportunities

The planning group evaluated their ministries for effectiveness. They determined that 88 percent of their active members were involved in parish-centered ministry (giving a total of 992 hours per week) and 11 percent (240 hours) to ministry beyond the church doors. While the percentages should have been closer to 80 percent internal and 20 percent external in a healthy congregation, the church's total number of volunteer hours exceeded the national average. The church facility was one of the finest in the Midwest and offered space for growth. Congregants were not content to reflect on the glory years but were seriously interested in doing what it took to reverse their negative trends. A Percept demographic study indicated that their neighbors were very open to family-oriented ministries. The church property had a fishing pond and acreage where the church could build a family life center, including softball and soccer fields.

Threats

Interest rates were at a historic high, so the church's debt limited their ability to launch new ministries. Employee morale was low because salaries and benefits had been cut. Church attendance had declined over a five-year period to an average of 740 and giving was down 50 percent. Demand notes were being called, which impacted cash flow. Population in the fifteen-mile radius around the church had been declining for ten years. The plan for a new highway, which was to open economic development for the northwest corridor, had been scrapped by the state. The church's governance structure was perceived to be dysfunctional.

Re-visioning

Through a time of prayerful discernment, this church clarified its vision for the future. They decided to focus on "being a growing community of believers involved in a ministry of reconciliation." The vision included the following actions steps:

- Begin a new approach to evangelism that was relational rather than confrontational.
- Flatten the organizational structure by developing a one-board governance system.
- Plant two new congregations in the next two years.
- Develop softball and soccer fields and engage the YMCA to use these facilities to nurture over 250 community children.
- Create a community-wide singles program to provide divorce recovery care, with financial counseling, for the growing number of single adults and children.
- Build Habitat for Humanity houses for low-income families in the community.
- Develop partnerships with inner-city churches to provide relief and development.
- Provide an alternative worship service, less formal and less traditional.
- Plan for citywide unity services across denominational and ethnic lines.

In the next five years, the congregation's morning attendance grew from 760 to 1,184. Two new churches were planted with a total of 212 persons in worship, bringing the total attendance of the three congregations to 1,396. While the mother church may never be as large as it was previously, their new vision for church health and multiplication has helped them fulfill the Great Commission and Great Commandments.

Building Bridges to the Future

Futurist Joel Barker writes, "More than anything else, leaders build bridges—bridges that help us move from where we are to where we need to be. Bridges made of hope and ideas and opportunity; bridges wide and strong enough so that all who wish to cross can do so safely."[24] Pastoral leaders can help congregations discover their identity and mission, then guide them to shape that mission in ways that are relevant and contagious. Church leadership is a spiritual practice that requires sensitivity and strength. The mission to make disciples of Christ is a noble calling and requires the best we can bring to the effort. There is nothing more rewarding than to help local congregations experience a renewal of evangelism and discipleship. Strategic planning, guided by the Holy Spirit, can help congregations become uniquely what God intended them to be.

24. Barker, *Leadershift*, 12.

Chapter Ten

Communicating the Gospel Publicly

John Paul II, in his papal encyclical *Redemptoris mission* (Mission of the Redeemer), insists that "preaching constitutes the Church's first and fundamental way of serving the coming of the kingdom in individuals and in human society."[1] More than thirty different words in the Old and New Testaments signify the task of verbally communicating the Word of God. The two terms most used in the New Testament are *kerusso* (more than seventy times) and *euangelizo* (more than forty times).[2] *Kerusso* means "to proclaim as a herald concerning a King or his decrees and *euangelizo* means to announce joyful news."[3] The abundance of different words regarding public speech implies that early Christian evangelists used a variety of approaches in communicating the gospel. It also suggests that preaching is a high priority of Christian ministry.

We know that several forms of preaching were used in the early church. Liturgical preaching was integral to the service of Word and table. Catechetical preaching attempted to ground new converts in the faith. The kind of preaching used to extend the community of faith was known as missionary or evangelistic preaching. Evangelistic speech, indicated by the Greek word *kerygma*, was known for its specific content and its inevitable conflict.

---

1. Martin, *Will Many Be Saved?*, 4.
2. Chapell, *Christ-Centered Preaching*, 96–97.
3. Ibid., 96.

Content of the *Kerygma*

1. The age of fulfillment has dawned.
2. This has taken place through the ministry, death and resurrection of Jesus.
3. Jesus has been exalted to the right hand of the Father as head of the new Israel.
4. The Holy Spirit in the Church is the sign of Christ's present power and glory.
5. The Messianic Age will shortly reach its consummation in the return of Christ.
6. The *kerygma* always closes with an appeal for repentance, the offer of forgiveness and the Holy Spirit, and the promise of salvation, "that is, the life of the Age to come to those who enter the new community." [4]

The Conflict of Competing Stories

When we speak of proclaiming good news, we imply there is some contrasting bad news. Indeed, a proclamation of the gospel often creates conflict because it calls for a demonstration of the love and justice of God for all people. Good-news preaching calls people to embrace the gospel as the story that best defines the totality of life. However, this good news of Jesus as Savior and Lord is not welcomed by all powers, principalities, and people.

Walter Brueggemann notes that public proclamation can be likened to a drama with three scenes.[5] In the first scene, there is a conflict between the forces of darkness and light. In the Hebrew Scriptures, this battle was often described as a struggle between the followers of Yahweh and Baal. In any meeting of adversaries,

---

4. Baker and Green, *Recovering the Scandal of the Cross*, 60.
5. Brueggemann, *Biblical Perspectives on Evangelism*, 16.

someone in authority may have to declare the victor. For example, in a sporting event, an official call often determines the winner and loser. Similarly, in spiritual warfare, God the righteous Judge determines the victor. In the ultimate biblical narrative, God declares that the conflict is settled through the death and resurrection of Jesus. Jesus is victorious over Satan, sin, and death (Rev 15:2–4).

In the second scene of the drama, an announcer describes what is taking place. The announcer narrates what is being seen and heard, using precise language to help people understand the struggle and the consequences of victory and defeat. The announcer does not determine the victor but rather reports with accuracy the verdict of the official or the judge. The announcer makes an overt verbal declaration regarding the outcome of the battle.

The third scene concerns the response of the spectators. Those watching and listening must decide whether they will trust the words of the announcer. Will they choose to embrace the declared significance of the contest—an event that happened in one time and place—and appropriate that outcome as the new reality that will determine the future course of their own lives?

First Kings 18:16–39 gives us an example of such a drama in the story of the contest on Mount Carmel. Yahweh's prophet Elijah encounters the prophets of Baal, and the narrator emphasizes that this is a winner-take-all contest. The announcer describes in detail what transpires and reports accurately the words of Elijah: "How long will you waiver between two opinions? If the LORD is God, follow him; but if Baal is God, follow him" (1 Kings 18:21). Yahweh the righteous judge determines the outcome by fire. The narrator then reports the response of the people: "The LORD—he is God! The LORD—he is God!" (1 Kings 18:39).

Through the millennia, people have read and heard this Old Testament story proclaimed. Preachers remind current hearers that what happened in the past has relevance for the present. They challenge people not to halt between two opinions but to choose God and denounce idolatry. Through this proclamation, people are brought to a point of decision. Some choose to affirm God as the center of their lives and others choose false gods. So the drama continues.

In the book of Acts, the gospel spreads through preaching that leads to conflict (Acts 13:43; 17:4; 18:4; 28:23–24). The missionary strategy was that apostles and other missionaries would go to local Jewish synagogues and preach the gospel. In most cases, the Christian preachers would be thrown out. Some hearers rejected the message and the messengers, but others responded positively to the gospel and followed the Way. Those who followed the Way of Jesus were incorporated into small house churches where bread was broken and the gospel was further explained.

Evangelistic preaching is hard work because it is not simply stating historical truth. For example, one can preach, Jesus is the way, the truth and the life (John 14:6). According to the witness of Scripture, this is a true statement. However, evangelistic preaching calls people to go beyond intellectual assent to personal repentance and commitment to follow Christ, which often results in behavioral change. Evangelistic preaching is not simply informational but always seeks to be transformational.

In the first century, the preaching of the gospel took place in a variety of places. As previously mentioned, Jewish synagogue guests were invited to read and comment on the Hebrew Scriptures each Sabbath. Followers of Jesus boldly accepted such opportunities. Often they would apply the week's text to remind their hearers that many of the Hebrew prophecies were fulfilled in Jesus of Nazareth. These evangelists then called synagogue members to put their trust in Jesus. For three decades Christian witness took place in Jewish synagogues before the door to public witness was closed.[6] Public proclamation also took place on the

---

6. Green, *Evangelism in the Early Church*, 301.

streets and in the marketplace. Christian evangelists simply took advantage of common daily gatherings to declare the message of Christ's victory. The book of Acts describes such open-air meetings in Jerusalem (2:5ff), Lystra (14:8ff), and Athens (17:17). Another important venue for the proclamation of the gospel was the lecture hall. Sometimes public speech as teaching overshadowed public speech as proclamation. An example of such evangelistic teaching was when Paul spent two years in Ephesus, having daily discussions in the lecture hall of Tyrannus (Acts 19:9). Michael Green identifies several schools where apologists for Christianity taught in the academy. He writes, "We must remember that these men were not dons, writing their apologies in safety and leisure. They were missionaries, preachers, evangelists and, in many instances martyrs."[7] Again, not all preaching of the first century was evangelistic. However, evangelistic preaching was vital to spreading the truth about Jesus and calling people to repentance and discipleship.

Planning for Evangelistic Preaching

Modern preachers need not and should not make every sermon evangelistic. The liturgical calendar affords ideal evangelistic preaching opportunities that are not forced or contrived, so evangelistic preaching should be intentionally scheduled throughout the church year. Consider the following opportunities for evangelistic preaching:

- Advent, the season of preparation and expectation, when sermons should instruct people to be ready for the appearing of the Lord.

---

7. Ibid., 314.

- Christmas, when we celebrate the joy that comes when we invite Emmanuel to be with us in good times and bad.
- Epiphany, which reminds the church that the gift of eternal life is not to be hoarded but shared.
- Lent, a season when we are reminded that unless we are willing to die to self, we cannot truly live.
- Easter, which celebrates victorious living now and in the life to come.
- Pentecost, which demonstrates the power of the Holy Spirit, who is available to purify and guide our lives.

Every season of the church year offers rich opportunities for evangelistic preaching. If you are called to the ministry of public proclamation, "keep your head in all situations, endure hardship, do the work of an evangelist, and discharge all the duties of your ministry" (2 Tim 4:5).

Public Proclamation Guidelines

Here are a few practical guidelines regarding evangelistic preaching in the local church and parachurch organizations:

1. Prepare yourself. "Preachers who do not address ethical concerns (personally and corporately) forfeit their ability to address evangelistic concerns."[8]
2. Prepare the congregation by establishing prayer teams who pray prior to and during public worship services.
3. Have congregational members regularly pray for family, friends, and associates who do not profess Christ.

---

8. Duduit, *Handbook of Contemporary Preaching*, 528. See also Long, "Faith Finding Its Voice."

4. Create public worship services to highlight conversions, baptisms, and transformational testimonies.
5. Determine specific calendar dates when evangelistic sermons will be preached.
6. Craft evangelistic sermons that call people to repentance and baptism.[9]
7. Extend invitations. Most people do not make a decision unless they are asked.
8. Be specific with instructions regarding what you want people to do with the invitation.
9. Do not manipulate or pressure people.
10. Remember the preacher is the second witness. The Holy Spirit brings people to Christ.

Recovering Our Nerve

In every age, evangelistic preaching has had its critics. Tertullian, the second-century father of Latin Christianity wrote, "We get ourselves laughed at for proclaiming that God will one day judge the world."[10] Justin, a second-century apologist and martyr, faced the same disdain from opponents who said "our assertions that the wicked are punished in eternal fire are big words and bugbears, and that we wish men to live virtuously through fear, and not because such life is good and pleasant."[11] You can expect to face opposition, too, some from within your congregation.

Motivations for preaching the gospel vary. Some preach out of obedience, others out of a sense of duty, still others out of a loving concern for the lost. In the end, "the proclamation of the Word of God has Christian conversion as its aim: a complete and sincere

---

9. See appendix 3 for an example.
10. As quoted in Green, *Evangelism in the Early Church*, 293.
11. Ibid.

adherence to Christ and His Gospel through faith...Conversion means accepting, by personal decision, the saving sovereignty of Christ and becoming his disciple."[12] How blessed are the feet of them who bring such good news!

---

12. Martin, *Will Many Be Saved?*, 4.

Chapter Eleven

Communicating the Gospel Personally

The public proclamation of the gospel through gifted communicators has been at the center of Christian faith and witness. However, the gospel was and is best transferred over time through personal conversations between family, friends, and acquaintances. Research continues to validate the fact that personal witness is the most effective means of evangelism.[1]

The historian von Harnack writes, "We cannot hesitate to believe that the great mission of Christianity was in reality accomplished by means of informal missionaries."[2] Jesus at his Ascension instructed his followers to be his witnesses as they went about their daily lives. Indeed, those who had witnessed the death and resurrection of Jesus could not keep quiet about this unique person and event. The followers of Jesus expected that soon and very soon, Jesus was going to return and establish his kingdom that would last forever and ever. This expectation consumed their lives and they could not help but speak about it wherever they went.

When Jewish believers were evicted from Jerusalem, they continued to talk about the Messiah (Jesus Christ) wherever their travels took them (Acts 8:1). Persecution did not silence their voices but solidified their resolve. Their widening witness went beyond Judaism and became multicultural when scattered Jewish believers began speaking "to Greeks also, telling them the good

---

1. Arn and Arn, *Master's Plan for Making Disciples*, 104.
2. As quoted in Green, *Evangelism in the Early Church*, 172.

news about the Lord Jesus" (Acts 11:20). It was in Antioch that this sect of Judaism began to take on an identity of its own, known as Christians (Acts 11:26).

Early Christian witness was effective because it was inclusive in word and deed. The radical nature of the Way did not exclude women, children, and slaves because Jesus had set a revolutionary example of including such folks. The gospel of Jesus allowed common folks to find a home and a place of service. However, the commonness of Christianity drew ridicule from religious and political leaders.

We witness an example of this contempt in a conversation between the second-century Christian theologian Origen and Celsus, a philosopher and opponent of Christianity. Celsus observed these informal Christian witnesses and sarcastically replied, "We see in private houses workers in wool and leather, laundry workers and the most illiterate and bucolic yokels, who would dare to say anything at all in front of their elders and more intelligent masters. But they get hold of the children privately, and any women who are as ignorant as themselves. Then they pour out wonderful statements: 'You ought not to heed your father or your teachers. Obey us…follow us…' With words like this they win them over."[3]

Although they ridiculed Christian witness, many political and religious authorities had to marvel at its authenticity and effectiveness. "When plagues brought death and desolation Christians cared for the sick while putting themselves at great risk. First and second century Christians welcomed women and children and took them in and granted them full fellowship and commissioned them to be prophets, apostles and teachers. It was inclusive love that drew in the disenfranchised and caused the elite to marvel at the love Christians had for each other."[4]

---

3. Ibid., 173.
4. Phelan, *Church in the Postmodern World*, 29.

Relational Evangelism

While first-century public witness centered in the synagogues and public squares, first-century personal witness was concentrated in households. Historian Kenneth Scott Latourette has observed that "the primary change agents in the spread of the faith were the men and women who earned their livelihood in some purely secular manner, and spoke of their faith to those whom they met in this natural fashion."[5] Both the Old and New Testaments note the existence of covenantal communities. These relational centers were known as *bayit* in Hebrew and *oikos* in Greek. These webs of influence were broader than mere blood relatives. They encompassed business associates, servants, friends, acquaintances, and extended family.

The gospel spread most effectively through these natural relationships. One day after healing a possessed man, Jesus told him, "Go home to your own people [*oikos*] and tell them how much the Lord has done for you, and how he has had mercy on you" (Mark 5:19). In the story of Zacchaeus we read, "Today salvation has come to this house [*oikos*]" (Luke 19:9). The *oikos* community was an effective place to share the message of Christ because people already had established trust relationships between themselves. These relationships allowed conversations over a period of time. The *oikos* also provided ongoing support for new believers.

Personal evangelism is most effective when we target our natural networks. Charles Arn, a church growth consultant, suggests that churches should strategically think about the effectiveness of natural relationships over against formal visitation programs since existing relationships are the most natural way to reach and disciple new believers. Boards, committees, choirs, classes, and small groups should consciously identify family,

---

5. As quoted in Arn and Arn, *Master's Plan for Making Disciples*, 39.

friends, and associates who do not know Christ. After a personal *oikos* is identified, a believer can look for opportunities to expose that network of friends to people and places where the gospel of the kingdom can be seen and heard.

Sharing the Gospel One on One

There comes a time in an ongoing relationship when opportunities arise to talk about spiritual things in a natural way. If we are open, the Holy Spirit will guide us to share the gospel and invite other people to believe. On such occasions, we can help someone move from being a good friend to becoming a good friend in Christ. Such evangelistic conversations take different forms. The following are a few examples:

Personal Testimony: When a spiritual conversation begins, it is often helpful to share your own testimony of how you became a Christian. Some testimonies are quite dramatic, as in the case of Saul's conversion on the Damascus road (Acts 9:1–9). Other testimonies are more commonplace, like that of young Timothy, who came to faith in a Christian home under the influence of his mother and grandmother (2 Tim 1:5). Each testimony is legitimate and gives evidence of the varied ways people are drawn to Christ. A personal testimony generally consists of three things:

1. My life before I became a Christian.
2. How and when I became a disciple of Christ.
3. My life since my commitment to Christ, highlighting successes and struggles.

Transformational Stories: Transformational stories describe God at work in our lives and in the lives of others. These stories often help people understand that God is not simply a cosmic Principle but a close Friend who works in our lives in memorable ways. In sharing transformational stories, keep these things in mind:

1. Be succinct. Share your experience in two or three minutes.
2. Be accurate. Do not exaggerate the story beyond belief.
3. Be specific. What spiritual lesson(s) have you learned?
4. Be thankful. When mystery appears, give thanks to God and treasure the moment.

Gospel Illustrations: In addition to your own testimony and transformational story, it is important to be able to summarize the gospel story of Christ and give others the opportunity to appropriate what God has done for them in Christ.[6] Most often, this personal appropriation takes place when people are asked the question, "Would you like to become a follower of Jesus?"

Rick Richardson likens the invitation to follow Christ to a dating relationship that leads to a proposal for marriage. Very few marriage proposals take place on the first date. Over a period of time, couples get to know each other by spending time together. They introduce one another to family members and friends. They explore their plans for the future. Words and deeds of love are expressed. After a period of time, a couple decides whether the relationship is going to move forward.[7] In North American culture, the man usually buys a ring and plans a special moment to ask the question, "Will you marry me?" The question is considered and then an appropriate yes or no (or "let me answer later") is given. If the answer is yes, then a wedding is planned, vows are exchanged,

---

6. See appendix 4.
7. Richardson, *Reimagining Evangelism*, 132–33.

and a wedding pronouncement is made: "I now present to you Mr. and Mrs. John and Mary Smith."

While there may be some flaws in this analogy, there certainly are some similarities between friendship evangelism and courtship. If we really care about our friends, there comes a time when it is appropriate to prayerfully ask, "Would you like to become a follower of Christ?" This is an anxious moment because we do not want our friend to reject the gospel and possibly reject us. It is also an anxious moment because our spiritual Adversary does not want this decision to be made. Regardless, we must be bold, ask the question, and trust God. If the answer is yes, we rejoice. If the answer is no, we continue to be an available friend.

In sharing the gospel, no precise words or scriptural formulas are appropriate for every situation. Several witnessing outlines can help you clearly present the message of Christ and state simply what you are inviting your friend to do. It is good to become familiar with several outlines that have been used successfully over the years. Some outlines are longer and more detailed, for times when an in-depth explanation is appropriate. Other outlines are so short they can be shared in two or three minutes.

There are a few questions to keep in mind when selecting or crafting your own witnessing outline:

- Does the outline focus on the person and work of Jesus as the basis for salvation?
- Does the outline emphasize the need for your friend's repentance from sin?
- Does the outline offer an opportunity for your friend to pray, confessing their sin and the need for Christ?

The Scriptures remind us there is great rejoicing in heaven when sinners repent and begin their new life in Christ (Luke 15:7). Evangelism in the twenty-first century will succeed when we who know Christ pray for opportunities to share the gospel with others, in word and deed. There is great joy in both the evangelist and the repentant when together they affirm, "The old has gone and the new is here!" (2 Cor 5:17b).

Chapter Twelve

Communicating the Gospel Corporately

A commencement address focuses on possibilities for the future. Graduates are reminded that their degree is not an end but a beginning. They are challenged to dream big dreams and do great things. Graduates then, often with great fear, launch out to seize opportunities and create new futures for themselves.

As the disciples of Christ were about to commence their mission, Jesus prayed to the Father on their behalf. He prayed that his followers might be unified in mission. In reflecting on what has been called the high priestly prayer, we see that it was a missional prayer. Jesus asked that his followers would have a unity that would accelerate evangelism. He said, "My prayer is not for them alone. I pray also for those who will believe in me through their message, that all of them may be one, Father, just as you are in me and I am in you. May they also be in us so that the world may believe that you have sent me" (John 17:20–21). Unity was not the objective of the high priestly prayer; Christ prayed for this unity among his disciples to draw men and women to himself. A united church in a divided world—that would be a wonderful evangelistic enticement. Jesus prayed that his followers might be one in spirit so they could fulfill their evangelistic mandate.

That the World May Know

A prayer for unity is one thing, but the practice of unity is another. James Earl Massey writes, "The spirit of unity...enables the believer to break free from patterns of selfish individualism and experience the fellowship that a common faith allows and shapes."[1] A church caught up in corporate individualism can become an inflamed fellowship easily enough, and improperly think such a holy huddle is the unity for which our Lord prayed. However, the prayer of Jesus was for a genuine love practiced in the corporate life of the church, which would draw diverse men and women to Christ and into responsible discipleship.

The unity that Jesus prayed for was not a uniformity of belief or culture. His goal was not to create a homogenized group of disciples. For example, Jesus did not pray for a unity only among Jewish men so that other Jewish males could be brought into the kingdom of God. Rather, Jesus prayed for a unity in the midst of human diversity so that people from every tribe and nation could be part of the one universal church of God. This unified church in a divided world would give witness to the intent of God for a new society.

The Ministry of Reconciliation

The apostle Paul was called to take this idea of a unified church beyond a sect within Judaism to all people and nations. His mission was to bridge the hostility between Jewish people, of which he was one, and all other people (Gentiles). His gospel call was to help all people understand how they could live in right relationship with God and neighbor. Regardless of class, gender, or race, the gospel maintained that all people were separated from God and each other. But through the death and resurrection of Jesus, a peace with God and others could be experienced and maintained.

But now in Christ Jesus you who once were far away have been brought near by the blood of Christ.

---

1. Massey, *Concerning Christian Unity*, 84.

For he himself is our peace, who has made the two groups one and has destroyed the barrier, the dividing wall of hostility, by setting aside in his flesh the law with its commands and regulations. His purpose was to create in himself one new humanity out of the two, thus making peace, and in one body to reconcile both of them to God through the cross, by which he put to death their hostility. (Eph 2:13–16)

This call—to restore the vertical relationship with God and the horizontal relationship with neighbor—was what Paul referred to as "the ministry of reconciliation" (2 Cor 5:17–19). The ministry of reconciliation understood that "all have sinned and fall short of the glory of God" (Rom 3:23). Therefore, all who hope to enter into the universal church of God need to experience the gift of God's grace through faith and not rely on human works (Eph 2:8–9).

In addition to this right vertical relationship with God, Christ called his church to sustain the horizontal unity between redeemed people. Members of the body of Christ do not create this unity but are called to maintain it (Eph 4:3). From the beginning, human beings were created to live in harmony with God, creation, neighbor, and self. Through the redeeming work of Jesus and through the community of the redeemed, God seeks to reconcile everything back to the original intent. As ambassadors of Christ (2 Cor 5:20), the church is called to seek peace wherever brokenness is found.

Curtiss Paul DeYoung points to one such ambassador of Christ who practiced the ministry of reconciliation. Rev. Lena Shoffner was preaching in a camp meeting in Alabama in the late nineteenth century after slavery had become illegal but segregation was not. According to Alabama law, whites and blacks could not worship together. During the camp meeting, a rope was stretched down the center of the tabernacle. Blacks sat on one side of the rope and whites on the other side. Rev. Shoffner talked about the middle wall of partition described in Ephesians 2:14, a wall that had been abolished in Christ. In response to her proclamation of the Word of God, people in the congregation took down the rope separating blacks and whites and gathered for prayer in the name of Jesus, the One who had called all of his people to dwell together in unity. When the surrounding community heard about this infraction of Alabama segregation law, they came with force to break up the camp meeting. Sister Shoffner's work was not the first or last time that people were persecuted for living out the powerful message of reconciliation in Christ.[2]

Signs of Corporate Unity in the Twenty-First Century

One of the greatest challenges and opportunities for the church in the United States is our nation's growing diversity. This challenge has a theological and practical component. Theologically, "it is one thing to conclude that racial prejudice and the discrimination that is causes are wrong and another to conclude that diversity is a theological virtue."[3] To theologically embrace diversity is to affirm that God created diversity and has called it good. From a theological perspective, churches will be biblically authentic when all kinds of people join together for common mission.

Since North American culture is becoming more diverse, congregations must be prepared to serve in multiethnic contexts. The United States Census Bureau estimates that by the year 2040, whites will no longer be the majority of the population in the United States. However, only 5 percent of congregations in the United States are multiethnic. A sign of genuine Christian unity will be seen when churches reflect the population change and intentionally move from being ethnically homogeneous churches to multiethnic churches.

---

2. C. P. DeYoung, "Biblical Reconciliation as 'God's One-Item Agenda.'"
3. Aleshire, "Gifts Differing," 6.

Another challenge for congregations of the twenty-first century is to base cooperative endeavors on our common experience in Christ rather than on common doctrinal convictions. There will always be differences of interpretation of Scripture, so churches must be willing to hold on to their understanding of truth with humility while extending a hand of fellowship to all who are in Christ. The evangelistic mandate is compromised when brothers and sisters in Christ refuse to extend charity to one another and minister together in harmony. A sign of genuine Christian unity will be practical cooperation between diverse denominations and movements in their evangelistic work.

Still another great challenge for evangelism in the twenty-first century is the opportunity to utilize all gifted evangelists. Scripture reminds us, "The harvest is plentiful, but the workers are few. Ask the Lord of the harvest, therefore, to send out workers into his harvest field" (Luke 10:2). A grand kingdom opportunity will be realized when all congregations recognize women as called and gifted evangelists. The urgency of mission must transcend gender bias and insist, "There is neither Jew nor Gentile, neither slave nor free, nor is there male and female, for you are all one in Christ Jesus. If you belong to Christ, then you are Abraham's seed, and heirs according to the promise" (Gal 3:28–29). An unmistakable sign of God-given unity will be our affirmation of all gifted evangelists, regardless of race, class, or gender.

A Reunion Metaphor

Jennifer Gooch was an art student at Carnegie Mellon University. She was from south Texas and discovered northern winters to be extreme. During her first winter, she observed many single lost gloves on the ground. She pondered the fact that a lone glove is useless without its mate, so "one lost glove" became to her a symbol for the sense of disconnect among Christians.

Out of her passion and creativity, Jennifer developed a wall space in her apartment where these lost gloves could be displayed. A friend helped her to launch a website, www.onecoldhand.com, where these lost gloves could be featured. Her mission was to unite the lost and found, in the conviction that "neither the loser nor the finder benefits," because both gloves are needed for proper warmth.

Onecoldhand.com can be a reunion metaphor for a divided church in a broken world. In order for the church to be an agent of reconciliation, we must practice a unity that transcends race, denomination, and gender. We really need each other. Every part of the body of Christ has a role to play in the Great Commission's evangelistic mandate. When a divided world witnesses a diverse church dwelling together in unity, their barriers of skepticism are lowered. When people outside the church see love in action, women and men are drawn to Jesus. Jesus prayed that we might be one so the world would know and believe.

Let the whole church say, "Amen."

Practical Steps
Toward Gift Discovery

Preparation for ministry in daily life involves many things. One crucial dimension of preparation is to discover spiritual giftedness. "Nothing would delight the heart of the Giver of life more than a huge unwrapping party. We determine our gifts, not by just trying to be a clairvoyant with God, but by examining our heritage, our situation, and our individuality."[1]

STEP 1. Examine the Scriptures

The first step in discovering your spiritual gift is to examine the numerous biblical texts on spiritual gifts. A partial list of spiritual gifts is provided in the manual *Discover Your Gifts*.[2] As you read through these working definitions and Scripture references, circle the response that is most true of you:

Leadership: The ability to lead members of a group with caring concern and foresight. "The exhorter, in exhortation; the giver, in generosity; the **leader**, in diligence; the compassionate, in cheerfulness" (Rom 12:8 NRSV, emphasis added).

(1)	(2)	(3)	(4)	(5)
Very little	Little	Some	Much	Very much

---

1. Hubbard, *Unwrapping Your Spiritual Gifts*, 19.
2. Shumate and Hayes, *Discover Your Gifts*, section III.

Shepherding: The ability to oversee the spiritual lives of others and care for their spiritual needs by teaching and guiding them toward maturity. "The gifts he gave were that some would be apostles, some prophets, some evangelists, some **pastors** *and teachers*" (Eph 4:11 NRSV, emphasis added).

(1)	(2)	(3)	(4)	(5)
Very little	Little	Some	Much	Very much

Teaching: The ability to communicate knowledge to others for the purpose of building them up. "The gifts he gave were that some would be apostles, some prophets, some evangelists, some pastors **and teachers**" (Eph 4:11 NRSV, emphasis added).

(1)	(2)	(3)	(4)	(5)
Very little	Little	Some	Much	Very much

Evangelism: The ability to present the gospel to unbelievers in a clear and meaningful way which calls for response. "The gifts he gave were that some would be apostles, some prophets, some **evangelists**, some pastors and teachers" (Eph 4:11 NRSV, emphasis added).

(1)	(2)	(3)	(4)	(5)
Very little	Little	Some	Much	Very much

Discernment: The ability to distinguish between truth and error, to know when a person or act is of God. "To another the working of miracles, to another prophecy, to another the **discernment** of spirits, to another various kinds of tongues, to another the interpretation of tongues" (1 Cor 12:10 NRSV, emphasis added).

(1)	(2)	(3)	(4)	(5)
Very little	Little	Some	Much	Very much

Encouragement: The ability to motivate people through encouraging words to live practical Christian lives. "The exhorter, in **exhortation**; the giver, in generosity; the leader, in diligence; the compassionate, in cheerfulness" (Rom 12:8 NRSV, emphasis added).

(1)	(2)	(3)	(4)	(5)
Very little	Little	Some	Much	Very much

Faith: The ability to envision what God wants to happen and to be certain the Lord is going to do it in response to prayer, even when there is not concrete evidence. "And if I have prophetic powers, and understand all mysteries and all knowledge, and if I have all **faith**, so as to remove mountains, but do not have love, I am nothing" (1 Cor 13:2 NRSV, emphasis added).

(1)	(2)	(3)	(4)	(5)
Very little	Little	Some	Much	Very much

Mercy: The ability to empathize with hurting people—that is, feel and sense their suffering—and to translate that into cheerful acts of service. "The exhorter, in exhortation; the giver, in generosity; the leader, in diligence; the **compassionate**, in cheerfulness" (Rom 12:8 NRSV, emphasis added).

(1)	(2)	(3)	(4)	(5)
Very little	Little	Some	Much	Very much

Healing: The ability to serve as God's channel in curing sickness and renewing health (physical, spiritual, emotional) through God's healing power. "To another faith by the same Spirit, to another gifts of **healing** by the one Spirit" (1 Cor 12:9 NRSV, emphasis added).

(1)	(2)	(3)	(4)	(5)
Very little	Little	Some	Much	Very much

Prophecy: The ability to proclaim and apply God's truth so that believers may be edified, encouraged, and consoled, and so that nonbelievers may be convinced. "To another the working of miracles, to another **prophecy**, to another the discernment of spirits, to another various kinds of tongues, to another the interpretation of tongues...And God has appointed in the church first apostles, second prophets, third teachers; then deeds of power, then gifts of healing, forms of assistance, forms of leadership, various kinds of tongues" (1 Cor 12:10, 28 NRSV, emphasis added).

(1)	(2)	(3)	(4)	(5)
Very little	Little	Some	Much	Very much

Administration: The ability to organize and guide human activities so that Christ's purpose is carried out. "And God has appointed in the church first apostles, second prophets, third teachers; then deeds of power, then gifts of healing, forms of assistance, forms of **leadership**, various kinds of tongues" (1 Cor 12:10, 28 NRSV, emphasis added).

(1)	(2)	(3)	(4)	(5)
Very little	Little	Some	Much	Very much

As noted earlier, this is only a partial listing of the New Testament gifts. While no single list in the New Testament is exhaustive, neither is any book written about the gifts.[3] However, gift discovery begins with a thorough biblical investigation.

---

3. Other helpful references are Carbonell and Ponz, *Uniquely You Growth and Ministry Profile*, and Earley, *Every-Member Ministry*.

STEP 2. Explore with Others

The second step in gift discovery is to talk with others who have discovered their spiritual gifts. Effective ministry requires friendly, functional connections with other ministerial colleagues. What better way to begin those connections than by initiating a conversation about your spiritual gifts? Schedule an appointment with several ministers in your area whom you would like to get to know, and ask the following questions:

1. How did you sense your call to ministry in daily life? What were the internal and external validations of that call?
2. What are your spiritual gifts?
3. How did you discover your giftedness?
4. How have you developed your gifts?
5. How and where do you use your gifts?

As you listen to the stories of others in pastoral ministry, your own gift discovery will begin. In turn, share the story of your spiritual journey with them. One of the most effective ways to pass on our faith tradition is through shared stories.

STEP 3. Experiment with Gifts

The third step in discovering your gift is through exploration and experimentation. Pray that God will reveal to you your area of giftedness. For example, through prayer and fasting, you may sense teaching is a special ability God has given to you. If so, then volunteer to teach a class. You may have received a blessing by helping others accomplish a task or goal, so you volunteer to assist someone with another effort. As you support them in their ministry, you may discover that you have the gift of helps. After prayer and study, you may recognize that you have an ability to organize and guide others in complex activities. If so, you could volunteer for an administrative assignment in vacation Bible school or some other ministry opportunity.

While God does not write our spiritual gift(s) in the sky, we can pray, study, and experiment with different gifts and ministries to discover God's direction in this respect.

STEP 4. Determine Effectiveness

The fourth step is to assess your effectiveness in a certain ministry over a period of time. Do not be tempted to quit too quickly. Simply because you have a spiritual gift does not exempt you from times of frustration in using it. If God has truly given you a gift, then you will be able to accomplish the ministry for which it is suited. In addition, you will have a sense of satisfaction in exercising your gift. For example, if God has given you a gift of teaching, then people will learn and you will find personal fulfillment through involvement in teaching ministry.

STEP 5 EXPECT VERIFICATION

The last step of gifts discovery is to listen to others who recognize and affirm your giftedness. Gift recognition requires mature listening skills, so do not rush around asking everybody whether they think that you are gifted in this or that. Rather, over a period of time, listen for affirming words from other believers who are spiritually mature. Confirmation may be as simple as, "Thank you for organizing this event; everything went so smoothly."

If you are experimenting with a gift of teaching, take to heart students' comments like, "That course had a life-changing impact for me." When they make such observations, the Holy Spirit may use that feedback to confirm your spiritual gifts.

SPIRITUAL GIFT DEVELOPMENT

After you have discovered your gift(s), begin to develop them. Most people who minister to others in daily life grow in effectiveness over time.

Seminars, workshops, and courses at the college or seminary level can help you develop your spiritual gifts. For example, if you have a spiritual gift of mercy, you may find that a course in missions education will make you aware of new ways to use that gift. If you have a gift of discernment, a pastoral counseling class may give you skills to use it most effectively. A spiritual gift of encouragement can blossom in a course on preaching, teaching, or gospel singing. The development of spiritual gifts requires discipline and determination.

The Holy Spirit apportions spiritual gifts to enhance congregational life and the community at large, so we should seek accountability for our use of these gifts. Both ordained and non-ordained ministry are connected to the church. In fact, those who perform their ministry in daily life have a dual accountability: first to God, the Giver of their gifts and ministry calling, and then to the church, which recognizes and supports both the minister and the gifts.

Gifts of the Spirit are absolutely essential for the health and development of the church, so it is tragic to see such gifts neglected. The parable of the talents is a warning of missed opportunity (Matt 25:14–30). "The gifts of God's Holy Spirit are precious and true. And the Lord of the church demandingly wants them treated as such. But they are neither like gold to be stored in Fort Knox nor like Rembrandt's painting to be hung in a well-guarded museum. They are fuel to be converted into spiritual power; they are seedlings, which will grow into fruitful trees; they are ore to be refined into useful tools. Any less profitable use of them will find the Master calling us to account." [4]

---

4. Hubbard, *Unwrapping Your Spiritual Gifts*, 88.

As ministers prepare for service, the discovery, development, and use of spiritual gifts is imperative. Why should discovery come before development or use? Obviously, it is difficult to develop or use a nonexistent or unrecognized gift. Many spiritual-gift inventories can help you begin the discovery process. Vocational counselors at colleges and seminaries are also available to help persons called by God to identify and develop their spiritual gifts for effective kingdom service. Unwrap your spiritual gifts and use them to the glory of God.

Appendix 2

ministry area profile 2012

Snapshot

Coordinates: 33:48.28 118:11.30
Date: 4/16/2012

Prepared For:
Your Organization Name Here
Your Address
Your City, CA 90001

Study Area Definition:
3.0 Mile Radius

Population and Households

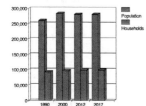

Primary U.S. Lifestyles Segments-2012

The population in the study area has decreased by 2686 persons, or 0.9% since 2000 and is projected to increase by 809 persons, or 0.3% between 2012 and 2017. The number of households has increased by 2081, or 2.2% since 2000 and is projected to increase by 1176, or 1.2% between 2012 and 2017.

Population By Race/Ethnicity-2012

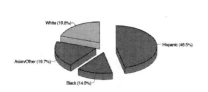

Population By Race/Ethnicity Trend

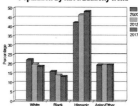

Between 2012 and 2017, the White population is projected to decrease by 2965 persons and to decrease from 19.8% to 18.7% of the total population. The Black population is projected to decrease by 1988 persons and to decrease from 14.0% to 13.3% of the total. The Hispanic/Latino population is projected to increase by 5575 persons and to increase from 46.5% to 48.4% of the total. The Asian/Other population is projected to increase by 187 persons and to remain stable at 19.7% of the total population.

Households By Income-2012

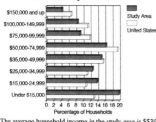

Population by Age-2012

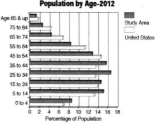

The average household income in the study area is $53913 a year as compared to the U.S. average of $67315. The average age in the study area is 33.5 and is projected to increase to 34.6 by 2017. The average age in the U.S. is 37.5 and is projected to increase to 38.3 by 2017.

(800) 442-6277 v21.1a

© **1990-2012 Percept Group, Inc.**
Sources: Percept, Nielsen, U.S. Census Bureau

ID# 283:17508

Page 2

Used by permission. http://docs.perceptgroup.com/pg/pdf/MinistryAreaProfile/
MinistryAreaProfile-LongBeach.pdf (accessed August 19, 2013).

105

We All Need Saving

Genesis 3:1–7; John 19:28–37; Revelation 5:6–10

Note: This sermon was delivered at the Anderson University School of Theology Miller Chapel on February 19, 2013.

The same simple phrase can signify the greatest delight or the deepest despair. For example, when a student submits the final paper for the final course in the final academic year, the professor may hear the exultant cry, "It is finished!" However, when a senior takes the required comprehensive examinations for the third and final time—and fails—"It is finished!" can be a cry of utter despair.

When Jesus spoke this phrase on the cross (Greek, *tetelestai*), onlookers undoubtedly understood it in widely disparate ways. Jesus' earthly friends heard "It is finished" and probably thought Jesus declared that his life was over. Religious and political enemies heard the same "It is finished" and relished the thought that a troublesome religious threat was now gone. The hounds of hell may have heard "It is finished" and declared final victory over God. They were all wrong.

John the Beloved gives us a clue to the meaning of Jesus' *tetelestai* when he writes, "Knowing that everything had now been finished, and so that the Scripture would be fulfilled..." (John 19:28). *Tetelestai* is translated here as "everything had now been finished," and it refers to the long series of events from Golgotha back to the garden of Eden.

Irenaeus, a second-century disciple of Bishop Polycarp, who is also believed to have been a disciple of John the Beloved, wrote that Jesus came to earth *to do again* what had been *undone* by our ancestors in the garden.[1] In other words, what had been undone in one time and place (Eden) had ruined lives around the world ever since. According to the Genesis hymn of creation, God placed Adam and Eve in a perfect place. God gave them everything and allowed them to tend and enjoy the garden. However, one day, "the tempter speaking through the voice of a serpent"[2] came to Eve and said, "Did God really say, 'You must not eat from any tree in the garden'?" (Gen 3:1). Eve said, "We may eat fruit from the trees in the garden, but God did say, 'You must not eat fruit from the tree that is in the middle of the garden, and you must not touch it, or you will die'" (Gen 3:2–3).

Picture it: In the garden stood a tree that God had placed off-limits. I suppose it could just as easily have been a lake, path, or mountain; Adam and Eve knew that everything in Paradise was available but this one thing. However, the serpent tempted Eve to doubt what God had said about it. "'You will not surely die,' the serpent said to the woman. 'For God knows that when you eat of it your eyes will be opened, and you will be like God, knowing good and evil'" (Gen 3:5). She took and ate the fruit and gave some to her husband. They must have turned to each other and said, "Look, we are still alive. The serpent was right. God was wrong."

However, something cataclysmic happened with that act of disobedience. Wanting to be like God (*sicut Deus*[3]), Adam and Even changed in a way that could not be detected by the human senses, a way that surpassed human comprehension itself; but

---

1. Green and Baker, *Recovering the Scandal of the Cross*, 119. Irenaeus wrote that Jesus "recapitulated"—that is, he did perfectly—what Adam and Eve and the whole human race had done imperfectly.
2. Bonhoeffer, *Creation and Fall*, 66–67
3. Ibid., 70.

the change was nonetheless real. As a result, Adam and Eve were exiled. It was finished. Paradise was lost.

But God was not finished with the human race. Though we live in the exile from Eden and Satan may "bruise" us, God promised that our enemy would be crushed (Gen 3:15).

You do not have to look very far to see the bruising and bondage that result when people doubt the word of God. Several years ago, when I pastored in Phoenix, Arizona, a young mother of two little girls (with a third child on the way) sat in my office. She had actually been in my office on two previous occasions, but each time she had abruptly excused herself before she could tell me why she had come. During the third visit, she told me she was trapped and needed help desperately. She told me her husband had left her, so she had no place to go and no means of support.

When I asked if she had family, she said she had run away from home at age fifteen. She did not know who her dad was, and her mother had physically abused her from the age of four. She was unable to open her hands because, at the age of four, she had gotten into some of her mother's things so her mom stomped on her hands, crushing the bones. She was never taken to the hospital, so the bones of her hands were permanently deformed. At fifteen, she had said, "It is finished" and run away.

Sometimes we need to be saved from our families.

While on the streets, she joined a church. One of the families took her in and provided shelter. Teenagers in the church youth group introduced her to illegal drugs, and she became a drug abuser. Because of her erratic behavior, the elders of the church made her to lie down on the floor at the front of the sanctuary, where they held her arms and legs and tried to force her into submission. The elders locked her in a room for hours at a time, punishing her for breaking church rules. When opportunity presented itself, she ran away. "It is finished," she said. She was done with church forever.

Sometimes we need to be saved from religious institutions.

I will never forget the night I was called to the hospital prior to the delivery of her third child. Our congregation had located an apartment and helped her with groceries. Some young moms in the church purchased linens for her; some elderly ladies cared for her children while she attended AA meetings. When I walked into her hospital room, she began to weep uncontrollably. The birthing team would be inducing labor soon, and she admitted that she feared for her baby. She confessed that she had not been attending AA meetings. When the ladies of the church sat with her kids, she slipped out and did cocaine with her friends. Now she worried that her baby might be addicted.

I tried not to show it, but I was angry. I felt used. I said, "How can you afford the drugs?"

She said, "My friends told me I could repay them later."

Sometimes we need saving from our friends.

The truth is, we all need saving.

Redemption (an image of commerce) is one of several biblical metaphors used to describe how the death of Jesus saves us. Other biblical metaphors borrowed from public life of the ancient Mediterranean world are "justification (court room image where a guilty person is declared, not guilty), reconciliation (image of restored relationships), and sacrifice (an image of worship). All of these metaphors and more are legitimate biblical images of how the death of Jesus saves us."[4]

I find it quite interesting that a church council was never called to determine which metaphor explains most precisely how the cross of Jesus saves us from sin. From a historical-theological standpoint, it appears that different metaphors had greater cultural traction at different times in Christian history.[5]

---

4. Green and Baker, *Recovering the Scandal of the Cross*, 23.
5. Richardson, *Evangelism Outside the Box*, 124.

In my opinion, redemption is still a worthy metaphor for the day in which we live, because our tolerant post-Christian culture has become somewhat squeamish about the penal-substitutionary idea of a wrathful God needing to be satisfied through the death of his Son. But redemption may strike a chord. Gustaf Aulen, the distinguished twentieth-century Swiss theologian, reminds us that redemption is perhaps the oldest metaphor used by the church to explain how Jesus saves.[6]

In both his life and death, Jesus played out the redemption story to the very end. The Gospel writers record the words of prophets and psalmists that foreshadowed God's Redeemer, from the detail of the vinegar (Ps 69:21) soaked hyssop plant (Ex 12:22) lifted to his mouth, to the reminder that none of the bones of the paschal lamb should be broken (Ex 12:46). The apostle John adds an important detail of this redemptive act: the fact that Jesus' death on the cross was voluntary. John writes, "With that, he bowed his head and gave up his spirit" (John 19:30). No one took the life of Jesus. Had Jesus desired, he could have called ten thousand angels to protect him from the Romans, the Jewish leaders, or any other enemy. Rather, Jesus gave his life as a ransom for many.

"The significance of the cross has become for many of us an obvious matter of theological affirmation."[7] We sing with great rejoicing, "What can wash away my sin?/Nothing but the blood of Jesus."[8] The story of redemption reminds us that what God created and called good was broken because of our wanting to be like God and doubting the word of God. The disobedience of our ancestors

---

6. Aulen, *Christus Victor*, xxi. Gustaf Aulen calls the redemption metaphor the classic idea that through the death of Jesus on the cross hostile powers have been defeated and humans redeemed.

7. Green and Baker, *Recovering the Scandal of the Cross*, 12.

8. Robert Lowry, "Nothing But the Blood," in *Worship the Lord: Hymnal of the Church of God* (Anderson, IN: Warner Press, 1989), 422, verse 1.

led to exile and bondage, but we too have transgressed God's law in word and deed. Like our ancestors, we are stuck in the grip of our adversary and cannot free ourselves. Like them, we are sometimes are blinded by our arrogance and do not even see the need for deliverance. Because of my sinful ways, I cannot redeem you, nor can you redeem me. We need a Savior who can set us free.

John the Baptist saw Jesus and declared, "Look, the lamb of God, who takes away the sin of the world" (John 1:29). John the Revelator saw the scene around the throne in heaven and heard the people sing a new song: "You are worthy to take the scroll and to open its seals, because you were slain and with your blood you purchased for God persons from every tribe and language and people and nation" (Rev 5:9).

When Jesus cried, "It is finished," whatever claims our adversary thought he had on us—whatever power he thought he held over our souls—were null and void. We were purchased with a commodity that only Jesus could pay. Mathew reports that when Jesus cried out, the sky grew dark. The earth shook. The temple curtain was torn in two. The graves opened and the bodies of holy people walked the streets of the city (Matt 27:45–53). Everybody knew this was not an ordinary execution; something big was going down. Indeed, the redeeming work of Jesus opened gates that had been closed for millennia and set us free.

On several occasions, I had spoken with Judy Wren, the young mother in my office. I helped her as best I could. I told her about God and how God could help her. But the pain of her past trapped her without hope for the future.

One day I invited a friend to meet with Judy and me. My friend was an elder in the church and a very successful businessman, the first African American to own a McDonald's franchise in the United States. By this time, he owned five. But his success led to access, and he became enslaved to money and drink. His wife had prayed for his redemption for years.

One Sunday morning, he was watching religious TV, waiting for an NFL football game to begin. The preacher was talking about the ability of Jesus to set people free. My friend had tried to start over several times by resolving to be a better person, but that Sunday morning he realized he couldn't do it on his own. He needed a Savior/Redeemer. Sitting alone at home, he asked Jesus to set him free.

Judy listened to his story. She saw a man who was once bound, now set free. For the first time, she realized there was hope for her—not only hope to be forgiven, but to be *set free*. Nobody needed to remind Judy of her brokenness. She knew that very well. What she needed was hope that things could be different. She needed to be set free. Charles Wesley expressed it this way,

He breaks the power of canceled sin,
He sets the prisoner free,
His blood can make the foulest clean,
His blood availed for me.[9]

When Pope John Paul II visited the United States in 1987, he held an evening mass at Sun Devil Stadium in Tempe, Arizona. The location of the meeting created much controversy. On most Saturday evenings during the harvest moon, devotees would gather outside Sun Devil Stadium to build fiery altars and sacrifice sow, cow, and fowl. Intoxicants flowed freely as fanatics clothed in cultic regalia were led in chants by scantily clad young maidens. The rest of the year, fanatic football fans sacrificed large sums of money each week to get close to their idols. When the Sun Devils prevailed on the gridiron, great blasts of fire would fill the sky to the cheers of the Sun Devils and their devotees. The Devils would

---

9. Charles Wesley, "O for a Thousand Tongues to Sing," in *Worship the Lord: Hymnal of the Church of God* (Anderson, IN: Warner Press, 1989), 77, verse 4.

cry, "We won! We won!" Then fans would pour out of the stadium and enter neighboring communities for a time of revelry.

Many religious leaders felt it was a bit unsavory for the Vicar of Christ to celebrate mass in the confines of that stadium, but John Paul II was not deterred. After all, this was a mass. In Latin, *mass* (from the phrase *ite missa est*) means the church is "sent forth into the world." The church on mission need not fear, for not even the gates of Diablo can divert her mission. [10]

The stadium was filled with believers and nonbelievers. Hymns, psalms, and spiritual songs were sung. Scripture was read. The gospel proclaimed. Pope John Paul II went down on the grassy field where the poor, the sick, the blind, and the lame were given preferential seating. The Vicar of Christ walked among the wheelchairs, anointing with oil and praying for all who had need.

Then the Pope blessed the bread and the cup. The elements were reverently distributed to seventy thousand worshipers. Immediately, after the bread and cup had been consumed, the sky was filled with fireworks that went on for five minutes to the amazement all who had gathered. Following the final burst in the sky, in a brief moment of silence before the applause of the crowd, a little child cried out, "We won! We won! We won!"

Christus Victor! We are free at last.

If you are not among the redeemed, then I invite you to acknowledge your sin, believe in Jesus as your Redeemer, and confess him as Lord. Join him in doing God's will on earth as it is being done in heaven.

---

10. Wright, *Meal Jesus Gave Us*, 36–37.

THE BIG STORY SHARING GUIDE

You should end up with something like the little picture to
the right, with four circles, matching the ones numbered
below, and on the next page. My directions are in bold
(so don't say them out loud!) and what you say is lighter.

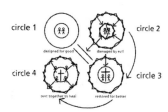

circle 1   circle 2

circle 4   circle 3

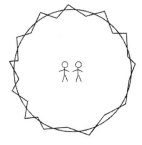

Start with circle 2 (our world without Jesus):

Draw outer circle. Tell me what the world is like.
Draw people. When you turn on the news what do you see?
Draw messy line as you give examples: Among all the violence,
and war and terrorism, and the AIDS pandemic and global warming,
you've got to admit that our world's pretty messed up.

What's interesting is how we feel about those tragedies. None of
us think that violence and disasters are good, and all of us long for
a better world. Our longing for a better world seems to point to
the fact that either a better world did exist or will one day exist.

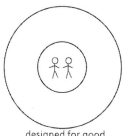

designed for good

Start circle 1 (original world with God):

Draw the outer circle. In the Christian worldview we believe
a better world did exist, and God designed the world so that
we took care of the earth and each other.
(Draw people) And our good care allowed the earth to flourish. And
above all, God took care of us and we blessed him through our obedience.
Draw inner circle, representing God's care.
God tells us that the world was designed for good.
Write *designed for good.*

Now, return to circle 2, and add more:

So how did the world get in this mess?
Start drawing arrows representing selfishness. Well, we decided that we were going to run the show. And when we started
putting our own needs above caring for other people or the planet,
we started damaging ourselves and everything else: the world,
(draw dividing line) our relationships with each other,
(draw inner circle and "scratch out") and ultimately we damaged
our relationship with God. The whole world had been damaged by evil.
Write *damaged by evil.*

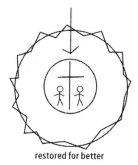
restored for better

Begin circle 3 (Jesus entering our world):

Draw outer circle with "mess." But the great news is that God actually loves the planet and us too much to leave us that way.
Draw arrow, draw cross. So 2,000 years ago, amid our brokenness, God came to live on the earth as Jesus.
Draw people. And during that time he started to teach us a better
way to live and began to tell us about this thing called the reign of God.
Draw inner circle. The reign of God is where all the good things
that are supposed to happen actually do happen. In order to bring
about God's reign Jesus died and rose again. In his death the damage that we caused in our lives, in our relationships and in the world
died with him so that, when he came back to life three days later, he
made new life possible for us, for the planet, and for our relationship
with God. That's what is great about the cross. It looks backward
and forward. We are forgiven for the damage we have done, and
we are also provided new possibilities for life as God designed it.
Because of Jesus the world is being restored for better.
Write *restored for better*.

Now, draw circle 4 (God's kingdom in our world):

Well then what's our response?
Draw outer circle with "mess." Even though God has done the hard
work, we still need to respond. This world is still messed up.
Draw cross, draw inner circle. But Jesus is starting a revolution.
Start drawing people. He wants us to join him in bringing about
restoration in our broken world, but we need to follow after him in
order for that to happen. What he's asking is for us to allow him to
heal us so that we can be sent together to heal.
Draw "sending" arrows.
Write *sent together to heal*.

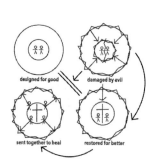
sent together to heal

Your circles are done. Now present the bigger picture:

Draw center arrow. Now, you might ask why I can't just jump
from knowing our world is suffering, to being the cure. Why do we
need Jesus to step in? Well remember how the cross looks both
backward and forward?
Draw side arrow. We can't move forward unless the damage we
have done is repaired. We need Jesus to forgive us and heal us.
Draw two lines. Plus the world's problems are infinite, and we
would get overwhelmed taking care of all the problems on our own.
Draw bottom arrow. We need Jesus' resources so that we can
become the kind of good we want to see on the planet. We need
Jesus to live in us and to lead us and that's crucial.

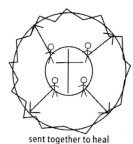
designed for good
damaged by evil
sent together to heal
restored for better

So where are you?
Circle 1: Are you here where you think the world is doing just fine?
Circle 2: Are you here, where you are completely overwhelmed by the
world's problems?
Circle 3: Or are you here, where you've got some sense of God working in
your life but you aren't involved in his mission?
Circle 4: Or are you here, where you are trying to make this world a better place
but have a hard time finding where God fits into the picture?
Where are you?

Response & Follow-up

The person identifies Circle One, *world is doing just fine,* as his or her response to your presentation. A follow-up question would be, *"Are you open to God showing you the mess that is in the world and in you?"*

The person identifies Circle Two, *overwhelmed by the world's problems,* as his or her response to your presentation. A follow-up question would be, *"Are you open to God showing you his answer to the mess in the world?"*

The person identifies Circle Three, *sense God is working in their life, but aren't involved in his mission,* as his or her response to your presentation. A follow-up question would be, *"Are you ready for Jesus to forgive, heal, and lead you in his mission?"*

The person identifies Circle Four, *trying to make the world a better place, but having a hard time finding where God fits in,* as his or her response to your presentation. A follow-up question would be, *"Are you ready to let Jesus lead you into a community that is working to bring healing to this world?"*

Taken from *Reimagining Evangelism Participant's Guide* by Rick Richardson, Terry Erickson, and Judy Johnson. Copyright © 2008 by Rick Richardson, Terry Erickson, and Judy Johnson. Used by permission of InterVarsity Press, PO Box 1400, Downers Grove, IL 60515. www.ivpress.com.

Appendix 4: The Big Story Sharing Guide

Bibliography

Adcock, Mark. *A Call to Grandparenting: Lessons Learned on Papa's Pond*. Anderson, IN: Warner Press, 2013.

Aleshire, Daniel O. "Gifts Differing: The Educational Value of Race and Ethnicity." *Theological Education* 45, no. 1 (2009):1–18. http://docs.ats.edu/uploads/resources/publications-presentations/theological-education/2009-theological-education-v45-n1.pdf

Anderson University School of Theology Faculty. *We Believe*. Anderson IN: Warner Press, 2003.

Armstrong, Chris R. "The Other 100,000 Hours: How the Church Marginalizes Itself from the World World." *In Trust* 24, no. 2 (2013): 20–23.

Arn, Charles, and Win Arn. *The Master's Plan for Making Disciples: How Every Christian Can Be an Effective Witness through an Enabling Church*. Pasadena, CA: Church Growth Press, 1982.

Aulen, Gustaf. *Christus Victor*. Eugene, OR: Wipf & Stock, 2003.

Baker, Mark D., and Joel B. Green. *Recovering the Scandal of the Cross: Atonement in New Testament and Contemporary Contexts*. 2nd ed. Downers Grove, IL: InterVarsity Press, 2011.

Barker, Joel. *Leadershift: Leaders Guide*. St. Paul, MN: Star Thrower Distribution Corporation, 1999.

Barr, David. *New Testament Story: An Introduction*. Beverly, MA: Wadsworth Publishing 2001.

Belcher, Jim. *Deep Church: A Third Way Beyond Emerging and Traditional*. Downers Grove, IL: IVP Books, 2009.

Bonhoeffer, Dietrich. *Creation and Fall*. New York: Collier Books, 1959.

Brueggemann, Walter. *Biblical Perspectives on Evangelism: Living in a Three-Storied Universe*. Nashville, TN: Abingdon Press, 1993.

Brunner, Frederick Dale. *Matthew, A Commentary: The Churchbook, Matthew 13–28*. Dallas, TX: Word Publishing, 1990.

Carbonell, Mels, and Stanley Ponz, *Uniquely You Gift and Ministry Profile*. Anderson, IN: Warner Press, 2012.

Chapell, Bryan. *Christ-Centered Preaching: Redeeming the Expository Sermon*. Grand Rapids, MI: Baker Academic, 2005.

Coleman, Robert E. *The Mind of the Master*. Old Tappan NJ: Fleming H. Revel, 1977.

Dean, Kenda Creasy. *Almost Christian: What the Faith of Our Teenagers Is Telling the American Church*. New York: Oxford University Press, 2010.

DeYoung, Curtiss Paul. "Biblical Reconciliation as 'God's One-Item Agenda': Broad Reflections on the Doctrine and Practice." Paper presented at the Global Forum of the Church of God, in Anderson, Indiana, June 2013. http://www.chog.org/sites/chog.org/files/documents/CurtissDeYoungPaper.pdf.

DeYoung, Curtiss Paul, Michael O. Emerson, George Yancey, and Karen Chai Kim, *United by Faith: The Multiracial Congregation as an Answer to the Problem of Race*. New York: Oxford University Press, 2003.

DeYoung, Kevin, and Ted Kluck. *Why We're Not Emergent: By Two Guys Who Should Be*. Chicago: Moody Publishers, 2008.

Diehl, William E. *Ministry in Daily Life: A Practical Guide for Congregations*. Herndon, VA: Alban Institute, 1996.

Duduit, Michael, ed. *Handbook of Contemporary Preaching*. Nashville, TN: Broadman Press, 1992.

Earley, Kevin W. *Every-Member Ministry: Spiritual Gifts and God's Design for Service*. Anderson, IN: Warner Press, 2013.

Faivre, Aleandre, and David Smith. *The Emergence of the Laity in the Early Church*. Costa Mesa, CA: Paulist Press, 1990.

Fee, Gordon. *The First Epistle to the Corinthians*. Grand Rapids, MI: Eerdmans Publishing, 1987.

Gibbs, Eddie, and Ryan K. Bolger. *Emerging Churches: Creating Christian Community in Postmodern Culture*. Grand Rapids, MI: Baker Academic, 2005.

Green, Michael. *Evangelism in the Early Church*. Grand Rapids, MI: Wm. B. Eerdmans, 1970.

Hubbard, David Allen, *Unwrapping Your Spiritual Gifts*, Waco, TX: Word Books, 1985.

Hunter, George G., III. *The Celtic Way of Evangelism: How Christianity Can Reach the West...Again*. Nashville, TN: Abingdon Press, 2000.

———. *Leading and Managing a Growing Church*. Nashville, TN: Abingdon Press, 2000.

The Interpreter's Dictionary of the Bible. New York: Abingdon, 1962.

Johnson, Jeffrey A. *Got Style? Personality Based Evangelism*. Valley Forge, PA: Judson Press, 2009.

Kinlaw, Dennis F. *We Live as Christ*. Nappanee, IN: Francis Asbury Press, 2001.

Kinnaman, David. *You Lost Me: Why Young Christians Are Leaving Church...and Rethinking Faith*. Grand Rapids, MI: Baker Books, 2011.

Kraft, Charles H. *Christianity in Culture: A Study in Dynamic Biblical Theologizing in Cross-cultural Perspective*. Maryknoll, NY: Orbis Books, 2005.

Kynes, Bill. "Postmodernism: A Primer for Pastors." *The Ministerial Forum* (Evangelical Free Church Ministerial Association) 8, no. 1 (Fall 1977).

Long, Jimmy. *Emerging Hope: A Strategy for Reaching Postmodern Generations.* Downers Grove, IL: InterVarsity Press, 2004.

Lyons, Gabe. *The Next Christians: Seven Ways You Can Live the Gospel and Restore the World.* Colorado Springs, CO: Multnomah Books, 2010.

Marsden, George. *Militant Christians: The Rise of Fundamentalism in American Culture.* Kindle Edition: Then and Now Reader, 2012.

Martin, Ralph. *Will Many Be Saved?: What Vatican II Actually Teaches and Its Implications for the New Evangelization.* Grand Rapids, MI: William B. Eerdmans, 2012.

Massey, James Earl. *Concerning Christian Unity.* Anderson, IN: Warner Press, 1979.

The Mission of an Evangelist: Amsterdam 2000 A Conference of Preaching Evangelists. Minneapolis, MN: World Wide Publications, 2001.

Nieman, James R., and Thomas G. Rogers. *Preaching to Every Pew: Cross-Cultural Strategies.* Minneapolis, MN: Fortress Press, 2001.

Phelan, John E., Jr. *The Church in the Postmodern World.* Fort Washington, PA: Christian Literature Crusade, 1999.

Phillips, Keith. *The Making of a Disciple.* Old Tappan, NJ: Revel, 1981.

Rainer, Thom S. *Surprising Insights from the Unchurched and Proven Ways to Reach Them.* Grand Rapids, MI: Zondervan, 2001

Rendle, Gil, and Alice Mann. *Holy Conversations: Strategic Planning as a Spiritual Practice for Congregations.* Herndon, VA: Alban Institute, 2003.

Richardson, Rick. *Evangelism Outside the Box: New Ways to Help People Experience the Good News.* Downers Grove, IL: InterVarsity, 2000.

Richardson, Rick. *Reimagining Evangelism: Inviting Friends on a Spiritual Journey.* Downers Grove, IL: IVP Books, 2006.

Schwarz, Christian A. *Color Your World with Natural Church Development.* St. Charles, IL: ChurchSmart Resources, 2005.

Schwarz, Christian A. *Natural Church Development: A Guide to Eight Essential Qualities of Healthy Churches.* St. Charles, IL: ChurchSmart Resources, 1996.

Shumate, Charles, and Sherrill D. Hayes. *Discover Your Gifts.* Anderson, IN: Warner Press, 1990.

Sider, Ronald J. *Good News and Good Works: A Theology for the Whole Gospel.* Grand Rapids, MI: Baker Books, 1999.

Sider, Ronald J. *The Scandal of the Evangelical Conscience: Why Are Christians Living Just Like the Rest of the World?.* Grand Rapids, MI: Baker Books, 2005.

Snyder, Howard A. *The Problem of Wineskins: Church Structure in a Technological Age.* Downers Grove, IL: Inter-Varsity Press, 1975.

Stephenson, Andy. *Smooth Hand Offs: Passing the Baton of Faith to the Next Generation.* Anderson, IN: Warner Press, 2012.

Tickle, Phyllis. *The Great Emergence: How Christianity Is Changing and Why.* Grand Rapids, MI: Baker Books, 2008.

Wagner, C. Peter. *Frontiers in Missionary Strategy.* Chicago: Moody Press, 1971.

Wijngaards, John. *The Ordination of Women in the Catholic Church: Unmasking a Cuckoo's Egg Tradition.* New York: Continuum Press, 2001.

Wright, Tom. *The Meal Jesus Gave Us: Understanding Holy Communion.* Louisville, KY: Westminster John Knox, 2002.

Name Index

Abraham, 3
Adam, 3, 108
Adcock, Mark, 50
Aleshire, Daniel O., 94
Alpha Course, x, 18–19
American Institute
    for Church Growth, x
Anderson University
    School of Theology, x
Anselm, Bishop
    of Canterbury, 31
Armstrong, Chris R., 48
Arn, Charles, 43, 63, 85
Arn, Win, 43, 63, 85
Augustine of Hippo, Saint, 26
Aukerman, John, x
Aulen, Gustaf, 111
Baker, Jon, 56
Baker, Mark D.,
    15, 76, 108, 110, 111
Barker, Joel, 73
Barr, David, 30
Belcher, Jim, 15
Bolger, Ryan K., 56
Bonhoeffer, Dietrich,
    2, 27, 108
Brueggemann, Walter,
    ix, 5, 9, 15, 76

Brunner, Frederick Dale,
    22, 25, 26
Calvin, John, 25
Campus Crusade
    for Christ, ix, x
Carbonell, Mels, 100
Celsus, 84
Chapell, Bryan, 75
Church at Brook Hills,
    The (Birmingham, AL), 27
Coleman, Robert E., 45–46
Cyrus, King of Persia, 16
Dean, Kenda Creasy, 56–57
DeYoung, Curtiss Paul,
    65, 93–94
Diehl, William E., 46
Earley, Kevin W., 100
Elijah (prophet), 77
Emerson, Michael O., 65
Evangelism Explosion, x
Eve, 3, 108
Faivre, Aleandre, 45
Fee, Gordon, 16, 18
Fischer, William G., xi
Francis of Assisi, Saint, 11
Gibbs, Eddie, 56
Gooch, Jennifer, 95–96
Green, Joel B.,
    15, 76, 108, 110, 111

Scripture Index